As WE Proceed ...

As WE Proceed ...

A Movement for the People

Kommon Knowledge

iUniverse, Inc.
New York Lincoln Shanghai

As WE Proceed ...
A Movement for the People

iUniverse books may be ordered through booksellers or by contacting:

iUniverse
2021 Pine Lake Road, Suite 100
Lincoln, NE 68512
www.iuniverse.com
1-800-Authors (1-800-288-4677)

Because of the dynamic nature of the Internet, any Web addresses or links contained in this book may have changed since publication and may no longer be valid.

The views expressed in this work are solely those of the author and do not necessarily reflect the views of the publisher, and the publisher hereby disclaims any responsibility for them.

ISBN: 978-0-595-46056-4 (pbk)
ISBN: 978-0-595-90355-9 (ebk)

Printed in the United States of America

To Eliese and the other women in my family,
for standing tall;
each of you like a statue of liberty to me.

Contents

Preface

Going through life is like being on a veritable "quest called knowledge". <u>As WE Proceed</u> chronicles my experiences while on that quest.

To expound, I believe that it is the desire of the people to know more about how the world works as well as how WE fit into that world which compels US forward and moves US onward; seeking clarity and wanting to make connections to what is known while questing for knowledge about what WE do not know. Fact is, while a few among US seem to have things all clearly connected, the majority of US will spend a lifetime seeking that knowledge.

Although this book reflects on my experiences of being Black and living in America, this quest is a common link which makes US all a sort of kindred folk. With that being said, I had to write this book as part of my quest.

I found it necessary to write down what you will read here so that I may clarify things for myself and make my own connections with the world as I am coming to know it. I found it necessary to speak out; verbalizing my thoughts and observations as well as some of my reservations and regrets about how things work in the world.

It is important to note that in this book "WE" not only refers to Black people in America, but to those of US who are poor and disenfranchised as well. The term WE includes anyone who has been shut out, cut off, or locked down. WE is not limited just to those of US who have been disenfranchised by the American criminal justice system or its corrupted political devices or its greedy corporate entities because I realize that many of US have shut ourselves out of our communities, cut ourselves off from our families, and locked ourselves down by the way WE think or how WE act. Still, there are those of US who suffer being shut out, cut off, or locked down as a result from our lack of thoughts and/or actions.

It seems equally important to note that while "US" is sometimes used in this book to refer to the United States of America, I often use US to make some of the same references as I do by using WE. Are WE not also of the United States? Therefore, the United States is also US.

Moreover, the term US refers to the poor people of the world; people who have been historically exploited and forgotten.

As a final note, I use WE and US in reference to *any* people who America and the industrialized world have tried to write out of existence in hopes of ridding themselves of the guilt from the crimes that they have committed through the colonization and imperialism of the past, present and future globalization efforts, and capitalism run amok.

My perspective is that of a Black man raised in poverty in urban America, so, perhaps my point of view may seem more congruent with the left side of politics and society. At times my viewpoints seem to range somewhere between favoring a socialist democracy and democratic socialism, both of which advocate for some reformation of capitalism.

While I am definitely not a Republican, I do not feel that the Democrats deserve a free pass. WE have not been done right by either group so both political parties are criticized as they relate to US within these pages.

I wrote this book because I am the people.

I am the father who has failed his family. I am the family that is one step removed from poverty. I am the alcoholic who fears a relapse back into the abyss of substance abuse. I am the Black man who is one mistake away from being locked inside a prison cell. I am the inner rage that lies dormant like a time bomb ticking within the city.

I am also the single parent who endeavors to never be just another dead beat daddy. I am also living testament to our socioeconomic evolution as a people from slaves to sharecroppers to shareholders. I am also the break in the addiction cycle that has eluded so many people in my family. I am also the incarnate of the promise that education holds for the youth in my community. I am also the compassion and generosity that transforms a mean mug and a clinched fist into a genuine smile and a warm embrace.

Indeed, I am the people and the people are me. In homage to the Black Panther Party and to other revolutionary movements aimed at turning things around, I proudly exclaim: "All power to the people!"

WE must uphold our communities by attacking poverty, treating substance abuse, promoting our families, and pushing education amongst our people!

I say, let US reform the system because WE can no longer just go along with status quo! I am well aware that many of our powerbrokers in government and the business sector actually prefer US to comply and conform in order to preserve status quo. See, when in the absence of conformity there is conflict. They do not want the people to begin thinking because thought is a precursor to action. They cringe at the notion of US revolutionizing things. But I say,

> *Revolution is a part of evolution.*
> *With revolution there is conflict,*
> *conflict,*
> *and more conflict.*
> *Some conformity.*
> *Some ex-convicts.*
> *And then more conflict.*
> *Some contents under pressure*
> *from being disregarded as something lesser.*
> *Status:*
> *2nd Class.*
> *Separate and Unequal!*
> *Therefore, the sequel of our evolution*
> *lies in revolution*
> *and conflict.*

The reader may not agree with what I say in this book and I am at peace with that fact. However, my hope is that the reader will see that what I am saying throughout these pages is in agreement with the myriad of philosophers, activists, historians, politicians, theologians, and social reformists. That is, if WE do not know where WE have been then WE will not know where WE are going. In exclaiming: "All power to the people", I also proclaim that knowledge is power. So, as WE proceed, WE need to apply the knowledge that WE acquire and use it to make a world that better fits US.

In closing, while it is true that writing this book was part of my quest, keep in mind that I am still proceeding onward and forward. My movement is on-going as I am coming to know more about how the world works as well as how I fit into that world. Remember that writing this book was just a stopping point on my quest; something akin to pulling over and checking a road map while on a long road trip. While this book chronicles my life and my experiences to this point, it also helps to give me some direction on where I am headed next. My hope is that something in this book causes each reader to think and that the result of thinking leads to taking action. It does not really matter whether something in this book empowers, angers, shames, or enlightens the reader. Just knowing that reading it has caused further thinking lets me know that my purpose for writing <u>As WE Proceed</u> is being fulfilled. Hopefully, with US all doing more thinking, WE may find some solutions and improve things. Please visit **myspace.com/aquestcalled-knowledge** to comment and to engage in further discourse.

Revolution comes and
fires carry colors of
rage. With media as the
stage, delayed
broadcast is gonna now
podcast originally
untelevised. And if the
revolution must have a
color then I know that

status quo?

CHANGE is gonna come

proceed

Enemy ME

Some may see
and think of me as some kind of ex-military
revolutionary.
Or an anti-establishment victim
who got caught up in the system.
Or a quasi-political, left-winged radical
but I merely advocate for politics that are practical.
My contempt and my mistrust
only makes me stand up for what is just.
So, I'm not a radical extremist seeking a final solution
although when I do talk of revolution,
its not a revolution in terms of tearing down
but a revolution in terms of turning around.
Seeking not to revolt but to revolve.
I seek solutions and resolve.
And I ain't been in the military
but I am militant.
Although I mean my fellow man no ill intent,
I seem to be the one they wonder and worry about
while I'm figuring out the way
the game gets played.
Because I don't have to be an ex-convict
released from a lengthy prison stint
to know that the prison industry complex
ain't but so complex.
Or that there is nothing but slave labor to see.
A perfect match for our slave mentality.

Free labor performed by a captive work force
with work forced in shops,
factories,
mills,
or on chain gangs
but with no choice.
Left with no voice
except for screams of pain, frustration, and agony.
The condition of my people remains sad to see
and I speak out on these things because you have to see
that corporate sponsorship
plus government censorship
equals the unsanctioned political debate
that gets discussed amongst cellmates.
Jailbait for the socially conscious.
Exposing the game.
Imposing the shame on their conscience
in avoidance of a war on being terrorized.
Like Apartheid but now somehow Americanized.
A veritable ethnic cleansing
and the mixed subliminal messages sending
an unwelcoming helping hand to the illegal immigrant
in a nation that was founded by immigrants.
Some came unwillingly and others were willing.
Contributing through the buying and selling and stealing
of our incarceration …
our revolution …
our service …
are all valued highly but also regarded as worthless.
Calling forth Black liberation from an unjust system.
An unjust decision
based on circumstantial mitigation
and subjected to litigation
for JoAnne Chesimard, Mumia Abu Jamal, and countless others.
Exiled or incarcerated sisters and brothers.
'Cause in the same spirit of heroism was terrorism
seen by the dawn's early light
but it was called an "eerie scene of a war zone" by some

and by others "a destruction site".
By any name, it is a rage against the machine called industrialization
with America held in contempt as an industrialized nation
and death rained down from above as airplanes crashed into buildings,
moving trucks filled with explosives killed children,
and anonymous bombing attacks delivered via U.S. mail
damned US all straight to Hell.
Home-grown, foreign spawned,
or sponsored abroad—
who is the real terrorist?
This Black man who ain't got shit?!?
Or that green eyed, star spangled beast?
I say, "no justice—no peace"
because that's the way America wants it.
She flosses and she flaunts it.
Unwarranted?
Undoubtedly,
but just in case you are still wondering about me
or what I am not.

As WE Proceed

As WE proceed …
WE return to the scene of the crime.
WE return to the dream in the mind
of judgment on content of character and creed
for our collective thought and actions based upon need.
Speaking out on racist, anti-Semitism
but with cynicism.
WE see social inequity
and, at times, WE just let it be.
Turning our eyes blind.
Trying to remove our guilt.
Only proving our guilt
or, in a sense,
disproving our innocence.
As we proceed …
WE abstain from alcohol and drug use
but WE continue our substance abuse
as WE ingest our nicotine and caffeine
producing adrenaline.
Firing off even more dopamine
for our already over sensitized sensory receptors
making our endorphins cry their secretions
like tears raining from orphans.
Seems WE are all addicted to something.
And some may be addicted to more than just one thing.
As WE proceed …
scientists and doctors study cancer

searching for an answer.
Questioning some cancer causing sickness
or some sickness causing cancer,
a positive ID
for AIDS/HIV,
or some other human engineered, man made diseases
while WE call on Jesus.
viral: Ebola
bacterial: e coli
As WE proceed …
in the midst of war and global conflict,
heads of state meet secretly and talk shit
all while trouble is brewing
and children play among rubble and ruins.
Not in a war zone
but in a neighborhood near home.
Historically denied an education
and history denies our education
while his story provides mis-education
as our own actions systematically deny US our education
and systemically WE tend to deny ourselves.
As WE proceed …
WE "cut taxes so WE could spend more of our hard earned cash"
on higher prices for gas,
utility bills, and credit card minimums.
Bill after bill comes with no end to them.
Paid those bills to the best of our ability.
Spent all the money on utilities.
Now our family has heat
but WE can't afford to eat.
As WE proceed …

un-CONS/TIT/U/TION-all

It was unconstitutional
so
amends were made for the 13th time.
Written in ink that is black as night but not unlike I am.
Three fifths were compromised.
You can read this with your own eyes.
Words like "We the people"
and "All men are created equal"
were somehow used
to exclude
and somehow meant to hurt me.
Divide by five and count off the first three.
The 13th amendment
was supposed to compromise and end it
using three divided by five.
In the year of 1865,
the abolishment of slavery and involuntary servitude
did nothing to abolish self serving attitudes.
While our founding fathers held "truths to be self evident",
who knew the tyrant they feared would become the president?
"Ensure domestic tranquility"?!?
"Secure the blessings of liberty"?!?
But three fifths ain't equal to one whole
when an entire Black man could be bought and resold.

The entire Black man was used and exploited
but only three fifths were counted with two fifths aborted.

pro-BLACK

As I remain pro-Black
for my brothers and my sisters,
for non thinkers
and non listeners …
Those who need it most,
seldom seem to want to hear it.
My lyrics
while socially conscious,
plain ol' common knowledge
on some pro-Black shit,
overtly politicized,
ridiculed and overly criticized
by some folks who ain't got shit.
No pot to piss in;
nor window to throw it out of.
No doubt, cuz, I got this.
They called for boycott and got US to hold out.
Black folks got sold out
as Black leaders got bought and paid for.
WE don't believe hype
but WE perpetuate stereotypes.
Although WE know that
being pro-Black
is so much more than afro picks,
nappy hair, and raised fists.
Embrace my Blackness?
It takes some practice

as WE must remain forewarned
against allowing our culture to conform.
WE keep fighting that.
No change.
Remain plain like white and black.
Sort of egocentric
about being ethnocentric.
Check out the face of racism?
Start out in the mirror and check out the face within.
So transparent and clear that its see through
a message but not for just he who
smiles in my face and then tries to fool me.
Behind my back I'm nigger, ape, coon, or moulie.
As yellow tape states "CRIME SCENE—DO NOT CROSS"
like dead bodies chalked off as a loss
lain slain among those
warriors who fell in urban jungles.
They'll pay more attention to what some of US have done
but ignore the neighborhoods where WE come from.
Yet and still, I will remain pro-Black.
From the words I pronunciate
to the words I annunciate
like I am pro-Black
but what *is* that?
Hotep
what *is* that?
A Salaam Alaikum
what *is* that?
Habari Gani
what *is* that?
Hu Jambo
what *is* that?
Power to the People
what *is* that?
Stay Black
what *is* that?

Slaves 2
Sharecroppers

From slave …
to sharecropper …
to shareholder …
WE evolve
as WE revolve.
And WE speak rhymes
'bout having 3 dollars and 6 dimes.
Sometimes predicting
what you're fixin' to see.
WE came 360 degrees.
Did somebody say revolution?
A natural part of our evolution makes US say, "Fuck 40 acres and a mule!
WE wanna bet the whole farm!"
So WE revolt and take up arms!
WE raise our Black fists but instead of violence
WE grow silent and WE act on stock tips.
As our Black fists take hold of the American Dream
WE squeeze our dollars,
making Washington holler,
and Benjamin Franklin scream.

Mental Messages
from Middle Passages

Beware of the company you keep.

Doing their dirty deeds got me shanked from behind …
left out there to bleed.
No justice …
there's just this.
Can't trust this
'cause it don't fit.
"Don't mind him 'cause his mind has been messed with."
But it still resides in US
so WE can't get past this.
The mental message
of the middle passage.

He keeps twin Glock 9 millis.
Not for them hillbillies …
but for his brothers.
He don't be dealing with no others.
'Cause that's the mental message
of the middle passage.

No matter Avenue or Boulevard.
Whether walking the tier
or out on the yard,
you wanna be brick hard

but you ain't even built like that.
"Man, don't y'know blood gets spilt like that
and niggas get killed like that?"
So, I keep it movin' out here in these streets
but reside in the 'hood
to rest with my peeps.
Leave you resting in peace
if you messin' with me.
I try to keep my peace
but I'm also known to keep my piece.
Also keeps me a Doberman.
Break in
and takin' my shit
… its over, man!

That's the damned mental message
of the middle passage.
See, WE very much
mistrust
those folks who are most like US
'cause that's the mental message
of the middle passage
and WE Black folk
can't seem to get past it.

(Can't Stand)
Inner City Heat

While I cannot stand this inner city heat,
I am unable to forsake the sights of the streets.
Seemingly, scenes blend seamlessly with inner city scenery.
Burned out buildings bring forth unborn dreams to me.
Black on Black crime 'cause within my neighborhoods reside
robbery, extortion, and homicide.
On toes hang yellow tags.
Cold bodies lay flat on metal slabs.
Bodies that were formerly outlined in chalk.
Sometimes this inner city heat just gets too hot.
Billions of brown bagged bottles rest in peace emptied.
Our plight dismissed as urban blight so simply.
Homeless folk manage to live just as simply
while extravagant urban lifestyles leave many destitute and empty.
I cannot stand this inner city heat.
Oppressive pressures press down on me and depress me.
Man made dilemmas perplexes and stresses me
Some of my closest peeps while professional and all degreed out
still live 'round here and they love to get weeded out.
But corporate policies are in place just to weed them out
and in time they'll be replaced so there is no need to doubt
why I cannot stand this inner city heat.
Flashing red and blue lights and sirens signify sightings of the police.
Harassment, intimidation, and profiling allow me no relief.
Caught dead to right in my 'hood accused only of being Black as my crime

but doing little more than residing in the wrong place while at the wrong time.
A few uniformed fools too ready and willing to prove
how they could give a fuck less about your inner city blues
or whatever troubles that you may be going through
while they are proudly wearing our best city blues
too willing to taze … too willing to maim …
for failure to comply when refusing to give them my name.
Rogue cops get off with no one else left to blame.
The more things change the more they stay the same.
And I just cannot stand this inner city heat.

Down and Out Never

Never did WE lay down.
Never did WE stay down.
WE was never way down.
WE was just sort of lowdown
until WE decided to throw down.
And WE wasn't really lowdown.
Just sort of on the lower side of things,
know what I mean?
WE never, ever had a doubt.
WE may have been down
but WE was never, ever counted out.

4 Real Wannabes

A young ghetto child
learns about manhood falsetto style.
Like the brown bag from an emptied liquor bottle,
inside all hollow.
Not unlike the inner city.
Enter pity …
guilt …
remorse.
With no recourse, there is no way out.
Sneaks out the crib at night.
Stays out.
As working men lay down,
block becomes playground.
On corners,
pee wees look out to warn US.
"A-yo!
Peep out shorty!"
He's 14 going on 40.
A for real wannabe.
Don't know what he's gonna be.
But everybody's eating.
Nobody's bleeding.
Wants to show that he got heart
while his heart is still beating.

Needs Dem Streets

All respect due to those WE have lost through violence.
In their remembrance, WE pause for a moment of silence …

Rather than fight against it, I decided to try it
and I just can't live way out in all of that "peace and quiet".
Don't get me wrong … its cool and all …
I mean … its kinda like going away to school and all …
but I need to see my share of daily urban drama and violence
and I need to hear police, fire truck, and ambulance sirens.
I need to know that the convenience of curbside service is there
and I need to smell the promise of life after death in the air.
I need to feel the radiance of that good ol' inner city heat.
In short, I need the life giving vibe that only comes from the street.

Q & A

Mr. President, some answers WE demand!
You are supposed to be in command of the land.
But now our confidence has been shaken
because WE had been mistaken.
None of US thought they would dare
attack US from the air.
But WE saw all of the flashes
and WE heard those loud crashes
as two of our buildings
turned into rubble
and ashes.
WE saw crowds of people
run and stampede.
WE saw people just lie there and bleed.
Now it appears that WE all share the same fears
and WE share all of these questions
that still remain so unclear
like *how did this happen to our beautiful land?*
These are some of the answers
that WE demand.

4 Fallen Heroes

1965
I was not even alive
when we rushed over to Vietnam
to stop the Communist regime and keep it calm.
See, the French went into Dien Bein Phu
like some goddamned fools.
So, from the City of Hue near Quang Tri Province
from the Ia Drang Valley up to the Central Highlands
Agent Orange
transformed
green into brown
while napalm maimed and disfigured civilian farmers and towns.
An Loc Village
suffered its share of innocent blood spillage
and when the Village of My Lai had a massacre of more than 300
and the Viet Cong held the Tet Offensive rather than being hunted
and the Marine artillery base camp at Khe Sahn
was seized by the NVA and Viet Cong
President LBJ faced making wartime decisions
101st Airborne Division
Hill 937
10 days of fighting
more than 400 wounded
46 US servicemen dead
and the look of disgust on our faces after being ordered to abandon the recently
captured hill ... priceless
Millions of Vietnamese nationals lied still and lifeless.

With any part of the conflict that could have been legitimized gone,
we stopped at the 17th parallel of the Demilitarized Zone.
We stood our ground and drew a line in the sand
and wherever the enemy could be found we fought them hand to hand
and though some soldiers fall as rallying Viet Cong ambushes bring violence
standing tall in A Shau Valley as King Kong were American Jolly Green Giants.
But still the NVA continued pushing southward from Hanoi to Da Nang and
Hue …
southward towards the Mekong Delta taking Saigon along the way.
And ye though we walked through the valley of the shadow of death
and though we searched and destroyed until not a Commie was left …
and even though we had pushed all the way north from the delta to the DMZ
and won all the battles we still came home empty.
Rewarded only with the ingratitude of an entire nation
fueled by their indifferent attitudes instead of parades and embracing
because some considered the sacrifices we made as something less than zero
and counted US out at roll call instead of playing Taps for fallen heroes.

Pluralisms of WE
(US Again?!?)

If WE
never have been free
then WE know not what freedom is
but WE know what freedom is not.
WE get so used to having nothing
that WE don't realize what we've got.
WE leave our families
to join the army …
travel around the world to see all that WE can see …
"be all that you can be" …
"aim high" …
"the few and the proud" …
"it's not just a job—it's an adventure".
Recruiters will tell US all of this shit just so WE will enter.
And WE may nod in agreement and say to them, "there it is …"
but having no idea, truthfully, where it is.
Dealing with what they dealt
then feeling what WE feel,
WE go out and WE deal
cold, black steel within an hour of chaos.
But with no payoff
and despite the hour,
it just might be
WE will fight for power
as WE fight those powers that be.

Our armed forces
forces unlikely choices,
sometimes silences innocent voices,
and sell US on unlikely dreams
promising but seldom seems to deliver.
Recruiting US niggers.
Uses US.
Abuses US.
Places US out on the frontline
as WE sign up one time,
sometimes twice, or even three times
with Uncle Sambo on that "I want you"
to join US
and be mine type of shit
while a flag draped coffin is all that WE might get.

Urban Voices

I had presumed myself as innocent
until I assumed my own guilt.
As illicit sins succumbed to deviant passions
in some manner, form, or fashion
I carried that same guilt built by a nation.
Making me guilty by association.

Compassionate-less conservatism won't let me forget
the countless young folk that are left
in places where no children can be found.
From systems devised in keeping them down
and after seeing and doing so much they are no longer children.
There is no innocence left in them for building.
The innocence within them has been lost.
A high price for them to pay is the cost
of becoming forsaken folk just like me
so reaching common ground seems just as unlikely.
Angrily yet meekly
some seem to speak to me
with strong urban voices
being forced into taking chances
and forced into making choices.
While for some
solemn prison songs
in desperate ghetto tones
are sung as I have done.

Many nearly never know
because WE grown folks nearly never show
that seeds sown as late as November
may still yield sunflowers a month before September.
For in truly knowing that, there exists hope.
But not ignoring that there may be fire where there is smoke,
becomes a reminder of undaunted hope for our lost innocence
in a world that often only offers, in a sense,
promises
of hopelessness
to the young folk WE are facing
which makes US all guilty by association.

BLACK GOLD GREEN

BLACK

GOLD

GREEN

Paying higher prices for gas
and disposing of disposable cash
is something to see.

Setting record profits for oil companies.

Rises in crude oil prices.

Rising energy crisis.

Economic theorists make their assumptions
on supply affecting the demand set by consumption.

Large profits for the minority
are made off of the majority despite our numbering in the millions.
Netting profits in the billions.

Lies made for American Big Oil and Arabians
while President Bush fronts on US like he is chasing them.
Doing a political balancing act
but literal talents he lacks.

As America's head statesman
discusses, deliberates, debates, and
decides what he tells US.
He sells US on $70 per barrel being normal for crude.
Justifying Middle Eastern business practices as shrewd
while the American citizenry gets taken advantage of
and WE get left finding someway to manage because
their deceitfully shrewd bargains
only increases their profit margins
and makes their black gold green.

Y'know what I mean?

Now Mama is left broken hearted. Another young child's life was snubbed before it started. He was one of those foolish sons written about by King Solomon in Proverbs 1. His baby brother went from youngest infant to ~~~~~ in an instant. And ~~~~~~~ to bear ~~~~~~~ a statistic. She beli~~~~ should bury the p~~~~~ opposite. An extremely high price

1ne Mistake Made

A good boy was raised
but he made one mistake.
Now Mama is left broken hearted.
Another young child's life was snubbed before it started.
He was one of those foolish sons
written about by King Solomon in Proverbs 1.
His baby brother went from youngest infant
to eldest child in an instant.
And his Mama hoped to bear a survivor not a statistic.
She believed the child should bury the parent not the opposite.
An extremely high price to be paid
by a son for just one mistake made.

Talkin' 'Bout a Revolution

Some were filled with Satan
and player hatin'
on playing fields that had been unleveled
by self serving blue-eyed devils
in a nation of billions and billions served.
So WE go out and WE spread the word
and facts about being Black.
Because it takes a nation of millions to hold my people back,
WE send forth one million and one raised Black fists
employing anti-propaganda and counter terrorist covert operative tactics.
Talkin' 'bout shootin' some when the revolution comes—
a final solution to get things done
and to accomplish whatsoever WE strive for.
The last man standing will be known as the soul survivor.

Negronomics 101

It seems that some
have their Master's Degree in Negronomics 101.
As WE configure and wonder
all kinds of combinations of numbers
where odds ain't that we'd won
but that we'd have fun.
It's sort of funny—
trying to win we'd spend a lotto money.
And what luck or what the fuck?
As white stars earn bucks
finding their pot of gold
in a cup of Joe.
With so many stars Black
why must Black bucks still lack
and just where the fuck is our Black Starbucks at?
'Cause we've got our degree in Negronometry.
We'll go to church
and give until it hurts.
Literally speaking
on Black families who ain't eating
but somehow they'll pay their tithes.
As tides turn
on money earned,
preacher man dresses nice and drives a new car.
He collects your last cent but barely knows who you are.
We'll put ourselves in a fix
to get the roof on the church fixed.

Or give our special offering for the building fund.
Hoping to rebuild our community while building none.
And we'll continue to go for it.
WE give up all of our money with nothing to show for it.
Except the fur coats, the gold rings,
the diamonds, and extravagant things
that WE provide for the culprit.
Some holier than thou fake profiting from the pulpit
off the theory of Negronomics.
And he ain't no husband nor father
but he will be a dead beat baby daddy
who don't pay his child support
but drives around town in a short body caddy.
Bustin' moves.
Sitting on gold Trues.
White rag top and gangster whitewalls.
On his baby girl's birthday he might call
or if he comes through
he usually just runs through.
Talking about this and that
with that damn Negronomic theory behind his back.
When he does call, he'll sometimes no show
but he thinks his child won't even know.
It ain't even funny
how he don't give his baby mama money
but he'll give her his share of Hell,
He'll spend his last dime on some weed
or a new pair of 12's.
He's a triflin' ass
But he learned that in Negronometry class.
And she ain't fooling me.
Got expensive jewelry;
$150 watch on her wrist.
$200 dollar pair of kicks.
She'll make ten but spend ten
and then …
have plenty of time spent paying the rent.
While she could have owned something

she don't own one thing.
She'll drive around a house note
or waste her hard earned money on gambling boats.
Home ownership?!?
She ain't owning shit!
No property.
Mad money made
but spent improperly by some
and taught in Negronomics 101.

What is a Black Panther?

Can anyone answer?
What is a Black Panther?
An animal that kills
or someone that builds?
And how come some are prophets of rage
but others profit from rage?
Do WE get played
like pawns for profits
or pawns for prophets?
Aren't some of us ignorant and uncaring
showing our "nigg-norance" while not sharing?
And speaking of "nigga-tivity"
but meaning no "dis-retro-spect",
is nigga our skin color or is a nigga our mindset?
And although some of us may be heavier than others,
aren't WE all considered to be brothers?
So, why do some see US as niggas instead of as brothers?
And does a nigga's complexion even come in our color?

Then & Now

That was then and this is now …

Now there is this "War on Terrorism"
Then, it was some kind of act of heroism
against the threat of spreading of Communism.
The ends justifying the means for going out and bombing them
are more than hypocritical.
Hustlers have often called it "a pimp game gone political."
Just like US Black folk are done wrong …
the same goes for al-Qaeda now and back then the Viet Cong.
And as the blood-money made exchanges hands,
innocents and Americans fall dead in foreign lands.
A young terrified soldier
following orders then forcibly told to
check in to the Hanoi Hilton for an extended stay
is not too much different than modern day Abu Ghraib.
So maybe to some now Osama Bin Laden
is not unlike Ho Chi Mihn from back then.
The only difference has been the passage of time.
Same never ending battle for hearts and minds.
Same atrocities were committed way back when.
Heinous war crimes now done to them because they were done to him.
But some will say, "That was then and this is now."
And you'll tell me that it differs how?
Back then WE killed some VC named Charlie.
Now WE hunt a turban headed man in the Taliban.
But they have nothing more than I do

and they want the same things from life too but they've been lied to.
Our Commander In Chief
sits on high and lies in the seat,
gets high, and relies on his beliefs
in a war that was based on lies and deceit.
Military intelligence is such an oxymoronic contradiction in terms
just like checking for Vietnamese Charlies while Iraqi oil fields burn.
Now there is Islamic Jihad and back then somewhere near Da Nang
roadside bombed, booby trapped lives are still claimed.
When our young American soldiers begin to see some commonality
asking "Will you stand with US?", will be answered with, "Will y'all stand by me?"
And when disheartened G.I.s come to let bygones be bygones
the impact will be felt from Baghdad to Saigon
and, perhaps, only at that time will you see how
that was then and this is now.

WE Serve Time

WE serve time
but instead
time should be serving US.

Futilely,
WE
hope to hold on
holding on to hope
for in God WE hope to trust.
Surviving by doing as WE must.
WE displace our blame
often claiming to have been framed
and the way that WE have come up
is what causes US to go down
through this sadistic
cannibalistic
24 hour a day showdown.
WE lose a little bit more of ourselves
each time the doors close on our cells
and inside here
WE cannot hide our fears.
So hope also becomes imprisoned
within them
and our hearts turn hard and cold like penitentiary steel.
WE abandon all hope when WE exhaust all our appeals.

It seems so unforgettable,

faceless,
and faithless.
Faced with
our unforgivable fate.

Finally accepting of the inevitable.

And instead of time serving US,
WE serve time.

Survival of the Fittest

It is
survival of the fittest.
Its going to be
them or WE.
Him or me?
He's comin' up on E 'cause only the strong survive
and there is a bounty on me …
wanted dead or alive …
Amerikkka's most wanted …
under stress
from being under arrest
over confessions often made while under duress.
Not to be confused of driving DWI
'cause Black folks get accused of thriving BWI
That's *Black With Intelligence*.
Our most credible evidence
is ruled inadmissible and irrelevant.
As judge, jury, and executioner
come with grudge, fury, and begins shootin' ya.
Protected by badges as blue walls remain silent.
Ignorant and uncaring to our hopeless calls until WE become violent.
As innocent bystanders can attest and bear witness
that it is merely a matter of survival of the fittest.

Extraordinary Negroes

Not merely everyday, ordinary people.
Some were heroes as well as "she-roes"
Extraordinary Negroes
in search of their lives.
Researching the lies told in history.
Bullshitted,
omitted,
or not even taught
in his story.

An Open Letter Str8 from the Belly of the Beast

A-yo! son,
put down your gun
and peep out what I'm sayin' …

At 6 o'clock in the AM
the cell doors slide wide open.
The CO's orders are spoken,
"Inmates step out …
stand on the line and clear count …
turn and walk the line …
you—face front …
the rest of y'all—follow behind!
Convict, keep walking!
Keep movin'!
No talking!"
No time for, "How you doin'?"
when you're just *doin'*
but you don't know *how*.
The line is headed for chow.
I got me a piece of steel
but I still don't got peace.
If I gotta shank a man I will
to survive another day in the belly of this beast

where only the strong shall survive
and costs get paid back with an eye for an eye.
I don't mistake weakness or kindness
'cause weak eyes have been blinded over simple dirty looks.
Or they get extorted for their commissary
and money off their books.
So, I just put my back against the wall.
I read,
and pray,
lift weights,
play basketball.
I keep to myself.
I don't ask for
nor accept anyone's help.
Still, the violence doesn't cease.
I can't rest in here unless I'm resting in peace.
But Hell is also waiting for me
with more beasts and demons and locked gates awaiting for me.
For now, I walk among my Hell inside of here,
walking along my tier
trying to show them no fear.
No truer living Hell
than living in a 9x12 cell.
Jailed with virtual geniuses behind these bars
with minds so bright they'd outshine the stars.
But our eyes, ears, and minds
are turned dumb, deaf, and blind
to the organized hustles and gang violence.
We see it but we exercise our right to remain silent
and to, therefore, remain alive
because snitches catch stitches,
or they get punked out like bitches,
or go through pain to survive.
I don't ask for any favors
except from my Lord and Savior
because the debts made,
the bets paid,
the black market and drug trade

are overseen by the crooked COs
and a corrupt warden.
So, my heart has been hardened
like this cold penitentiary steel.
Cold.
Hard.
My soul scarred.
Left with nothing but time for me to heal.
But it is the very same time that serves you still.
Put down your gun.
Don't do as I have done.
I hope that you will avoid mistakes
and avoid this place.
You still have a chance.
You still have a choice
to not let locked bars and gates
silence your voice.

Hood Rich

Its all good?
But think how good it could get.
Get hood rich
in the entrepreneurial spirit.
No need for help.
Go into business for self.
Prescribe some self help.
Fuck a shirt, a suit, a tie, and all.
Sell street pharmaceuticals
delivered curb side.
Cannabis herb tried.
Smoking grooves and broken rules.
Laws broken.
Jaws of justice clamped down but jaws broken.
Chances taken?
"Chances took," answers crook who wants to get hood rich.
Now,
who wants to get
hood rich?

What is a NIGGA?

A nigga:
Why is he
considered by some
a conundrum
or an enigma?
Is he
100% crazy
or ½ man ½ amazing
in his game?
There is no shame.
He did something
but hid nothing.
He did something but did **not** think.
Is his mentality criminal?
Or is that reality subliminal?
Define it?
Is he criminal minded
or just another young, gifted, and Black mind
with Black thought wasted
on Black on Black crime?
Is he an entity
or an end to me?
Good riddance?!?
Identity hidden
or hidden identity?
Has it been revealed
or is it concealed

and carried in the small of the back?
Does he fall through the cracks,
get buried,
and end up underneath
like underground movements?
Six feet deep.
Is he African American?
Or an African in America?
What
is a nigga?

Black P.A.N.T.H.E.R Defined

Revolution … the sudden upheaval
  of status quo.
Revolution … the opportunity
  to rebuild our communities.
Revolution … the movement
  towards needed improvement
despite somewhat standing still.
And our struggle continues
as the term *Black Panther* is broken down into
Black **P**ublicist
Black **A**narchist
Black **N**ationalist
Black **T**errorist
Black **H**edonist
Black **E**volutionist
Black **R**evolutionist
We've been all these things
but still it seems
that WE can't be all things to all people.
Separately treated unequal.
Infamously endowed by Our Creator with certain inalienable rights,
WE the people, retain the right to protest and to fight.
Like Hampton,
Seale,
Carmichael,

Cleaver,
and Newton's
revolution
Promises **A**nother **N**ationwide **T**ime-bomb **H**aving **E**xplosive **R**epercussions
and is no longer left open for discussion.
Like Garvey's *Back to Africa Movement* to return to our ancestral homeland
but still not knowing where the fuck WE were going.
Like Black nationalists …
black Afro picks with fists …
WE went from Africa
to America
to indentured servitude
to enslavement
to emancipation
to Jim Crow
to Negro Codes
to Civil Rights
to Black Power
to economic empowerment,
political action, and social inclusion.
So, please, pardon the intrusion but the journey still continues
'cause WE are somewhat standing.
Still,
our struggle continues.

Motherland

I am a manchild on a search.
I am the firstborn grandchild of Mother Earth.

I am the son of my Afrikan Motherland.

She was raped by other lands.

I am her bastard child
away from my home and acting wild.
I am but one of Amerikkka's many stepchildren.
I am rep building on our legacies of lunacy.
I am soon to see Armageddon.
I am GREEN and BLACK and RED and
WHITE
and BLUE
and
I am stars
and stripes
and
I am fighting you.

I *am* the battle for my soul.

I am a son
involved in a fight his with father
for control.

Afro Rican

I am not just an
African in America.
Nor merely am I an African American.
But apparently I am African.
And inherently I am partly Puerto Rican.
I am definitely American.
Defiantly, I am American.
So, refer to me as an
Afro Rican.

(Black Maled)
A Prior Conviction

Black male
6'1"
215 lbs.
WE see him around.
He comes down and hangs with US.
Considered to be armed and dangerous;
but he is only armed with intelligence.
There is proof and evidence
that he carries a concealed history.
He is also known to carry concealed misery.
But he has no prior convictions.
He just fits the description.

WE Came to Protest

WE came to protest
unholy American
war ties
based upon lies,
half-truths,
and manipulation.
Perhaps
dividing US
as a nation.
Not anti-American soldier;
just
some exposure
on what is
unjust.
WE came to protest
taking a stand
opposing
the taking of
Afghanistan
and atrocities
committed upon the Iraqis
as war crimes.
WE protest
as the world watches
and hopes
while 15 foot bomb craters smoke.
Dilapidated buildings

are as devastated
as the lives of children
when hope becomes
abandoned
in places like Kosovo,
Qatar,
Darfur,
and Detroit.
Rogue governments pillage,
and plunder,
and exploit.
So, WE protest
with abortion rights,
versus pro-choice,
against pro-life.
And
as if someone had heard me say,
"Look, here comes the gays …"
But
is this my protest?
Is it theirs?
Or ours?
United
by stripes and stars
as one nation
coming to protest.
Hollering headlines
made for the media.
Holding
picket signs
while holding the lines.
Gathering.
Crowding.
Chanting and shouting
at our protest.

call for boycotts and protest on some
pro-Black shit. Criticized as being a
wannabe Black Panther creates more
problems than answers. But whether
over reacting or covertly acting
behind the scenes as mindless fiends
who blindly help the rich get richer,
as bullshit gets thicker the drama
varies from social to political
commentary on our state of the union
as a nation of Black folk. And perhaps
more of US need to over react so WE
can all become a nation of Panther
wannabes instead of doing nothing.

Protest

OPPRESSION

speak out

proceed

Why Not Boycott?

Take a moment to think about all that you've got
and then tell me why WE shouldn't boycott?

Due to the sacrifices of a few, look at what has been done.
WE all enjoy the benefits of the sacrifices that were made by some.
The folks in the 1960's knew that things could not stay the same.
So, they boycotted as an effective means for change.
But now since you refuse to stand beside US
Perhaps it is you who should be seated at the back of the bus.

Why not boycott?
The city has had no problem collecting our tax dollars.
Their problem is that they ignored our protests and hollers.
Or they appointed some do little committee.
Or they formed a do nothing commission that really works for the city.

And so, I ask you: why not boycott?

That was a revelation back in 2001.
Once again many have benefited from the sacrifices of some.
Civil unrest led to a revolution brought on by the youth.
They were disenfranchised and fed up from not getting the truth.
But they were guided by a fundamental belief:
"If there is no justice then there will be no peace".
That was their youthful cry behind the riot.
But the city offered neither justice nor peace—they only wanted quiet.
And as the whole world watched to see what you know who would do,

they saw that instead of change he wanted to "get back to business as usual".

So, why not boycott?
Some fires were set and there was some looting
but that happened after another questionable police shooting.
Then some more rogue cops responded and acted like fools.
And did you forget that unequally enforced nighttime curfew?
Like separate but equal or even Jim Crow.
The Cincinnati Negro—where the fuck can he go?
"Uh—excuse me … that is ours and that's ours too
but here are a few crumbs that WE have leftover for you".

Why not boycott?
If WE do not stand for something
then WE will fall for anything.
WE must realize that WE have control
and say so over the dollars that WE hold.
So, that is why I must continue saying,
if you keep spending your money the same way then you'll keep getting the same
thing.

And so, I ask you: why not boycott?
Now take a moment to think about all that you have not
and then please tell me why WE shouldn't boycott?

2 Wannabe Gs

When they see Crips ... they bust lips
And if he is a Piru ... well, he can die too
There is plenty of shit talk
pointed stars, hooks, and pitch forks
5 points or 6 points or hollow points
blunts or joints
40 oz beers and liquor
psycho killa or maybe something sicker

complicated daps and intricate hand signs
spray cans denote changes in battle lines
badlands stand in between
the streets can be unforgiving and mean
where waving false flags
gets you punked like fags
black hearts and tattoos
red juxtaposed against blue
most break North when some break left and others are broken to the right
preferring to shoot instead of fist fight

"tha thug life"
living trife
Hollow pointed Teflon bullet
Niggas behind triggers ready and willing to pull it
pistol packing YGs ... young menaces to society
too ready to smoke me ... never grow to be an OG
Which direction should you walk towards?

Gangsta Disciples or Vice Lords?
Peoples or Folks Nation?
"Punk ass mutha fucka … why you hatin'?"
Was it the Rollin' 60s, 70s, or 80's who shot at me?
¿Quieres rojo o azul, Papi?
Mi gente del barrio viejo contigo
Mobbing deeply wherever we go con mis amigos

But a true man can stand on his own
And he walks his road alone
So, he needs no clique
Because he doesn't talk shit
And he doesn't act shady
So, he carries no .380
He carries no 9 double m
Because he doesn't bring the trouble to them
And he finds no honor in being called an OG
Because he knows that there are better things in life for him to be

They Don't See

Why does this apply to me?
When I apply to be
some corporately conformed employee,
there are so many things that they don't see.

They've seen my brothers serve time;
wasting away their young, creative Black minds.
They'll see my strong Black hands
and then imagine seeing me stick it to "The Man".
They may see a kufi
or dashiki
and think of Carmichael
or H. Rap Brown
before they turn me down.

Because that is all they may want to see.

But the one thing that they won't see
will be
me.

Ghetto Child

Ghetto child
Out here runnin' buck wild
Runnin' amok now …
Wondering what the fuck now?!?
He is born of the streets and raised by the system.
Considered an assailant in as much as a victim.
Young life filled with drama.
The streets are his Mama.
The system is his father.
Deadbeat daddy don't even bother
to nurture his own ghetto child.
Coming into his own all alone and all on his own.
Nurtured only by the streets until he is full grown.
He embraces urban reality as cold hard fact.
He loves the streets and the streets love him back.
'Cause amongst the cold, hard stares
and "I don't give a fucks" and "I don't cares"
is acceptance and props and much love;
nothing but hugs
for the ghetto child.
So, next time that you see
a young thug rockin' a long white tee,
shoe laces draggin',
and oversized pants saggin',
doo rag or hat to the back
just bear in mind a matter of fact:

That ghetto child that you see …
He may have been me.

Only Just Bill

Well, he was Just Bill.
He was only Just Bill.
But y'all fucked with him on Capital Hill.
While y'all should have just left him alone.
Living in glass houses and throwing stones.
Wrongly thought that his reputation couldn't handle
an impeachment off some weak ass sexual scandal?!?
Publicly funded
with motives that were privatized.
Two consenting adults' business being publicized
by private I's
for the American publics' eyes.
And Just Bill said the same as most other guys:
"I did not have sex with that woman … Ms. Lewinski …"
He tried to lie fluently
to get the cameras out of his face
and to get the special prosecutor off of his case.
Ken Starr,
the big spender.
A special prosecutor with a special budget
to check up on who's fuckin'.
*69ing and redialing 1–900 numbers
on partisan politics and blunders.
That old foagie
wondering who got sucked
and who got stuck with a stogie.
But he was Just Bill.

He was only Just Bill.
And he still
came out on to top
of Capital Hill.

Naw! America the Beautiful Ain't My Mama

America the Beautiful is not my mama
'cause her drama ain't necessarily mine
Only my Motherland
can truly understand my conviction
with no commission of a crime
but can you spare a dime for a brother, man?
One thin dime
My "high" cost of care
Obliged to spend time in foster care
Like a foster child in some group home
My roots gone
Orphaned
Abandoned
Alone
Done wrong then isolated over in some corner
Told to make myself at home and then treated like some foreigner
Wondering, "where is my mommy?"
and "when will she come back over and get me?"
from this orphanage called America
Woke up and there I was
America's adopted son
No where to hide ... no where to run
Searching for my mommy to question this robbery

and unwanted legacy that slavery gave to me
The misery-go-round of Trans Atlantic triangular trade
of flesh for iron, silver, and textile goods made
slave markets profitable, invaluable commodities
and slave markets unstoppable, inhumane oddities
bondage sisters and brothers
forced labor grew tobacco and cotton
as others died aboard slave ships forgotten and rotten
from Senegal,
Angola,
Nigeria,
and Ghana,
Sierra Leone,
Liberia,
and Botswana
Chained together by twos in dark, filthy holds
Chained together by you to be bought and resold
Surviving one nightmare only to endure another
America the Beautiful has never been my mother
She let some former Confederate folks
become Ku Klux Klan with white hoods, robes, and cloaks
Crosses burned with vigilantism
used to justify Black lynchings
those who enforced the laws unable or unwilling to do their jobs
simply succumbed to the will of lynch mobs
Blacks dragged from county jails
often lynched right outside of their cells
seldom tried
rarely convicted
No! America is not my mother!
Enraged
Upstaged in Black face
Hapless characters represented my race
Twisted forms of ordinary American humor
Grotesque caricatures helped to spread racist rumors
Half moon smiles with saucer sized lips
Bulging eyes
Prancing

Dancing
Frolicking fools
Wheeled about
Turned about
Did jis so
And ebry time they wheeled about they jumped Jim Crow
Sambo
Aunt Jemima
Uncle Remus
Amos 'n Andy
portrayed penniless yet hopeful sharecroppers and mammies
While their modest portrayals reinforced notions of white superiority
and our roles were reduced due to lack of priority
Being given menial jobs as servants and cooks
still seemed the same to some as vagrants, derelicts, and crooks
Hell naw, y'all!
America ain't my mama!
Oh! What the fuck is this?
A raised Black fist?!?
The power to build or used for destruction?
Holding onto that power but still holding on to nearly nothing
'Cause like I said, only my Motherland
can truly understand my conviction
with no commission of a crime
you can be a first time felon
a third time loser,
a career criminal,
or a petty crime and drug abuser
and still be considered my sister or brother
but as for America the Beautiful
YOU
will never be considered my mother!

Chicago 8 (The Panthers Partied at the DNC)

History has recorded what WE have done here.
Somebody had to protest
and to become dissident.
Showing some dissent
in order to get treatment
that was decent
because other brothers
seemed to vanish
or they got to steppin'
like someone had brandished a weapon.
While some of US displayed this powerful, Black bravado
shouting out "Black Power!" as our motto
whether dark skinned,
light skinned,
or mulatto.

Preferring Black Nationalism
rather than Black nihilism.
Realizing that, by any means,
what this really means
is that WE no longer would be taken for granted
because once united then WE just wouldn't stand for it.
A Democratic National Party

pulled along by its purse strings
seemed to always leave US out cursing
but with no way to stop it.
Just holding US hostage.
Not treating US equal.
The least of two evils.

But WE have come from
hearing "Die Niggies!"
to putting on dashikis
and folding five fingers into our palms.
Closed tightly.
Most likely upraised
and then placed
into the air.
Now knowing that history will record what WE do here.

Skepticism or Wisdom (Jesus is Black)

Is it science or religion?
Based on fact or based on fiction?
Judeo, Christian, and Islamic revelations
versus scientific observations.
Doubt from skepticism
or doubt from wisdom?
As science challenges our spiritual being
because seeing isn't always believing.
In The Code of Hammurabi, The Rosetta Stone, and The Dead Sea Scrolls
who knows exactly what has been written?
The semantics may be hidden
within those words from the Torah, Bible, and Qur'an in their original script.
They read the manuscripts but skeptics still have their hands full
refuting His skin the color of burnt brass and hair like lamb's wool.
See, Sura 3 and Chapter 1 in the Book of Revelations
teaches us against those white washed, blue eyed conceptualizations.
My people, we've been through this.
Just read Chapter 11 in the Book of Genesis
to prove that Our Lord is a man of color.
A Black man like me—
and no other.

Hey White Tee

Fuck
what
they say
or what he say she say
'cause this is what
WE say …

I stare back into the face of society
defiantly
saying do not judge me
for wearing my long white tee.
I just might be
someone with a Ph. D, an M. Ed,
or several other college degrees.
I will rock my white tee
fitted ball cap and Nikes.
Hey whitey
don't prejudge me
or rub me
the wrong way
and don't say
WE are all alike.
Where WE come from
same are some
while others unlike.
But so long as you
choose only to view

my skin color and this urban uniform
white tee
jimmies
and backwards ball cap worn
then you may never see
and to you I may never be
a man like you
and you may never trust me
although you must see
that I will do
as any man must do.

N.I.G.G.A. Defined

WE Black folk use the word NIGGA as a term of endearment but what does it
mean?
The history and the socio-psychology behind that word remains for US to be
seen.
See, sacrifices that "niggers" made back then allows US to make it now …
So, please allow me the opportunity to break it down:
No other race has had to face the
Indignation and degradation that was
Given to US right in our faces and yet WE have been
Growing and prospering all the while
Enduring and contributing along with a smile to all
Races including our own
while at the same time WE were being robbed of all the culture that WE have
known.
Never
Ignorant
Getting
Goals
Accomplished
but so many of US are amazed and astonished
'cause WE still can call each other NIGGA.
Don't y'all folks know that
no one
has had so much stolen from them
and then have been forced
to do so much
with so little

for so very long
only to end up contributing
so much more
despite
merely being given credit for having done
so much less???
But all some are able to see is a NIGGER
and WE
still can call each other NIGGA.

Back Home

She abandoned urbanized metropolitan areas
preferring back woods and small rural towns.
Smoothly paved interstate highways have succumb to dirt roads
and red clay roadsides.
I am bound by blood and history to traverse hundreds of country miles.
Where former field hands forfeited fortunes.
She spent nearly four decades up North only to decide
beyond the Mason-Dixon line is where she will finally reside.
So we carried her back home.
Where cotton, corn, and 'cane reign king.
Where huge harvested fields mingle with the horizon.
As far as the eye can see.
A day filled abundantly
with cruel irony.
The weather was pleasant and fair that day
yet no eye was found tearless.
They all came to mourn
before continuing on.
Offering my family
condolences and sympathy.
Mama's body lied lifeless and empty
but those flowers were so beautiful.
And so was she.
Resting peacefully.
Buried
in the good company
of other lost loved ones dearly departed

in the family cemetery
adjacent to the churchyard.
Distant memories of them recently revisited.
Thoughts of times not so long since forgotten
and the sound of my daughter sobbing
was all that could be heard
over the reverend's last words
for my Mama.

As HE Remains

No matter
Jehovah
or Jah.
Allah,
or Yah
or Yahweh.
What I say,
it matters not
who He
might be.
As He shall remain
The Almighty.

Bombingham Back in '56

One struggle for one people.
WE were separate but not equal
in 1956 as Birmingham
became Bombingham
because southern Jim Crow segregation
meant degradation,
humiliation,
and intimidation.
Bethel being bombed by Bull Conner
and the fireman's fire hose
as the policemen fired at those
who defied dogs,
and made stands,
and faced Klans
but still remained nonviolent.

Gonna Do What I Gotta Do

I'm a ain't got
that
if left up to some
will probably have none.
But I am aggressive and ambitious.
Get wit' this ...
I am just like you.
I want something out of life too.

Haves and have nots
turned have mores and ain't gots
or won't never haves
So I go out and I grab.
Get me a ski mask
and refuse to ask
for what I can easily take away from you.
Don't make the mistake
of taking me too lightly.
See, I gotta eat nightly.
And this cruel world ain't quite right to me.
But it forces me
to do what must be done.
Remember that
as you stare back at the gun.
And I despise the fact

that I must take away from
someone who looks just like me
and probably just wants
the same things from life as me too.

Please, forgive me Lord for doing what I gotta do.

WE (Our Precious Time)

Our Black experience is about struggle
and overcoming that struggle in order to uplift
and overcoming that struggle despite conflict
and overcoming conflict, self hate, and mistrust.
Coming together to do as WE must.

Some chose death when faced
with
choosing slavery
or
remaining free.
Others waited patiently.
Bidding their precious time.
Knowing that
WE were truly
the best of our kind.

WE
have been
freed
yet
WE
remain enslaved
emotionally
as well as

socially.

WE
use the term "nigga" for each other.
WE
diminish the fact that WE are brothers.
WE
choose instead to assimilate with others
or
WE
commit black on black crime
or
WE
idly waste our precious time.
WE
refuse to learn from our mistakes and to see the point
so
WE
keep spending our best years inside the joint

or
WE
waste our precious time away on street corners
and
WE
spend our money with foreigners.

WE
have been physically freed
while
WE
remain in a state of slavery.

It is a slavery of the mind.
It is something that
WE
have lost
and for some reason

WE
are unable to find.
But some say, "if you free your mind then your ass will follow."
So,
WE
need to be spending our precious time like there will be no tomorrow.

WE
have come from
separation
to
emancipation
to
segregation
to
partial participation
and
some type of simulated assimilation.
Despite the best efforts of a culture devised upon our degradation
and
our humiliation.

Yes, WE
have arrived
(at least in our minds).
And it has *only* taken us 400 years of our precious time.

WMDs

WE ain't have to search the middle east for WMDs.
WE had weapons of mass destruction right here on these streets.
More appropriately known
as weapons of mass *self* destruction
upon further discussion.
Whether we're killed by a roadside bomb in Iraq
or killed by some home grown sponsored terrorist attack.
WE can get killed by a roadside bomb that some Arabs have in store
or get some bomb ass killa on the side of the road by some Arab store.
Ignorant and blindly searching for WMDs over in Iraq
like fiends and addicts search for weapons of mass self destruction right down the
block
And, irregardless of
killing for a "just cause"
or killing "just 'cause",
in either case, dirty money gets furnished for blood
through weapons of mass distraction,
mad illusion,
misdirection,
and much confusion
because crime, AIDS, and poverty
bothers me as the other true weapons of mass destruction
and WE potentially mistook that
our president had US bushwhacked.
With political heat now
having our nation facing a critical beat down,
WE close the borders.

WE usher in a new world order.
But what's really on order is a change of plans
as dirty money gets washed clean by a change of hands.

Constitutional Crises

My fellow Americans, WE
just might be within a Constitutional crises.
Once more an election has been stolen.
Our Head of State to corporate heads is beholden.
While WE have been lied to …
our young folk in Iraq have had to die too.
Our lack of checks and balance
ruins and wrecks our talents
as a country.
Cruel ironies that somehow only some see.
Right winged conservatism …
Republican regime, them folk from the church, and them …
Is this a democracy or is it a theocracy?
Or is it a breeding ground for hypocrisy?
Those damned Republicans …
out here causing US trouble again.
Congressional filibustering blues …
they can't win at the game so they want to change up the rules.
That's what it seems to me like
when oxymora roam free like
political science
is somehow used to justify political violence
that is committed by nothing more than political tyrants
conveniently covered up by political silence.
So, once again O Beautiful has turned ugly.
Blue states and red states are referred to so smugly.
Republicanism rearing its ugly head is too revealing

of the ignorance in the votes cast by some 48 million
ignored and disenfranchised
destitute, impoverished poor guys.
And despite how spacious our skies can be
this Constitutional crises determines how gracious our land can be.

In Just US WE Trust

Only some see
that for US niggas, time is money.
WE pay out our legal fees
as lawyers and district attorneys bargain
speaking legalese and technical jargon.
Politicians shake hands while politicin'
but become lawmakers that don't listen.
So, WE get caught up if WE are Black
and in possession of a vial of crack.
Another brother sent to prison.
Another god fell before he had arisen.
Sat in court with his mama, step daddy, daughter, and baby mama with him.
Sentenced to five years for just one gram of crack cocaine
but Caucasians with powder don't get the same.
Equally ironic as it is interesting
that the disparity in Amerikkka includes criminal sentencing.
My brothers and sisters, I can't seem to get this
when motioning the judge for separation of witnesses
that suffer from blindness, deafness, and amnesia
but still manage to testify at their leisure.
Some become mute.
All morally destitute.
Metaphorically as well as historically,
change
remains our only constant.
So, Black folks be warned
only a Negro complies and conforms.

Motherland Afrika

Whispers heard upon Serengeti winds.
Timeless journeys with no end.
Vast blue skies.
Black skin
that has been
sun-dried.
Fleeting grains of Saharan sands.
Emptied hands
attempting to grasp
akin to attempting to ask.
Opening a clenched fist which has held onto nothing.
Our lack of knowledge of self is equally troubling.
Yet our thoughts often flow freely like the waters of the Nile.
So Motherland Afrika remains life giving and fertile.
She has given birth to US all.
WE have risen.
Like the cascading mists rising above Victoria Falls.
Kindred sisters and brothers yearn.
They beckon.
They call.
For US all to return.

Justifiable Democide

They can't possibly know what it means to me
'cause ill gotten ends can't justify the means to me
which means our foreign oil dependency
doesn't justify the ends to me.
As the wild west meets
the middle east,
rising crude oil prices
increases our energy crisis
yet once again the vets get stuck
while VA benefits get cut
as hospitals close
and health care bills get vetoed.
Our economy turns upside down
as political rhetoric gets tossed around
to America's lost loved ones.
Here the blood comes
as Lady Liberty cries,
over 2,000 of her young sons die,
and countless more are wounded and maimed.
Unknown soldiers …
anonymous and unnamed.
Counted out by some as zeroes
by forgotten promises made to fallen heroes.
And when it ends they still won't know what it means to me
cause their ill gotten ends won't justify the means to me.

The Legacy of
Slavery from A to Z

From Ashanti to Zulu

WE spoke words of Swahili
but who knew
that WE would be
stripped
from her arms
by foreign hands
and taken far away to foreign lands?

From Ashanti to Zulu

WE had definitive cultures
and markets of trade
but who knew
that WE would be robbed of our language and culture
and then made
to assimilate
(but not truly)
and to participate
(but not fully)
in accordance to The Constitution
with no recognition
for our contributions?

From Ashanti to Zulu

Who knew
that the stolen legacy
would send forth me?

Freedom, Censorship, or Death

The freedom for say so
is a high price to pay for
censorship
but giving up free speech is an expensive gift.
Speaking constitutionally,
WE
still retain
the right to remain
silent.
Our freedom to be quiet.
So why not
exercise our freedom to boycott?
Or the freedom to riot instead of being quiet?
Or the right to become violent instead of being silent?

Wannabe Black Panther

Peace be unto The Movement.

To Kwame Ture,
Assata Shukur,
Mumia Abu Jamal,
Jamil Abdullah al-Amin,
and my other
sisters and brothers,
As-Salaam Alaikum.

"Wa-Alaikum Salaam" the answer is going to be
as this Black Panther wannabe
is expected to over react quick,
call for boycotts
and protest on some pro-Black shit.
Criticized as being a wannabe Black Panther
who creates more problems than answers.
But whether over reacting
or covertly acting
behind the scenes on mindless fiends
who blindly help the rich get richer,
as bullshit gets thicker
the drama varies
from social
to political commentary

on our state of the union as a nation of Black folk.
And perhaps more of US need to over react so
WE can all become a nation of Panther wannabes
instead of doing nothing.
Instead of talking shit to me,
peep history:
Bobby Seale made it the "Chicago 8".
And they stirred things up at the Democratic National Convention in 1968.
<u>If They Come in the Morning: Voices of Resistance</u>
was written by Angela Davis.
She was a Communist.
Influenced by Maoists,
they labeled Huey P. Newton as Marxist-Leninist.
Richard Aoki was a co-founding Black Panther and Japanese activist.
See, ain't no mystery within our history
but when WE become hopeless and helpless,
WE become self destructive.
But inside all oppressed people
are wannabe Black Panthers trying to get out.
America is a nation of wannabe Black Panthers just dying to be let out.
And that Negro-like complacency
masked by the face of criticism
breeds the sort of cynicism that WE need to get out.

Hell & High Water

Hurricane Katrina came Hell and high water 'cause New Orleans had both.
The government had boats.
Fact is, the government had votes.
While all WE had were signs that read: "HELP US."
Our government said, "to Hell with us."
They failed US.
And President Bush was the one to blame.
President Bush was unashamed.
He hid nothing.
Just stood there and did nothing.
Days short and dollars later Bush tried to fix blame.
A "full and thorough investigation" he claimed.
WE took one look
and read the guilt on his face.
What a disgrace!
Ignoring his lies and attempts at deceit
like he ignored our cries as the floodwaters ran deep.
Investigate who?
Department of Homeland Security?
The FEMA Director?
The guy on the Weather Channel?
Some safety inspector?
A scapegoat
some small guy …
go after the small fry instead of frying the big fish
despite what WE witnessed.
WE should have learned from Bush

but once again WE got burned by Bush.
Investigate who?
Like fierce winds blew from Hurricane Katrina
our discontentment grew
and our attitudes lingered
while the president pointed his finger at everyone else …
anyone but himself …
he even pointed at the people wanting help.
Compassionate-less conservatism is so troubling.
Like talking loud and saying nothing.
Talked so loud only he heard himself speak
while our rapid deployment division was delayed for nearly a week.
Elite 82nd Airborne Division
caught up in bureaucracy and indecision
while George Bush flew high overhead in Air Force One
not setting one foot in New Orleans until the blame game had begun.
Damn that man!
Damn Bush once again
'cause America has been AMBUSHED!
Ambushed once again.

I Be Hustlin'

I be hustlin' while Grandma turns a blind eye.
Used wack amounts of dope
cut with Arm & Hammer
and burnt a blind guy.
Done my dirt with young guys.
Dirt done in front of young eyes
like my little cousins' and brothers'.
Absentee baby daddy
and young mother
on lock down
or strung out.
On corners where WE hung out,
m'man cut a deal then he sung out.
A bitch ass nigga
turned snitch ass nigga.
Dropped dimes on who shot who
and spoke on who pulled which trigger.
But with no evidence,
when it comes to gettin' dem Presidents,
the word on the street becomes irrelevant.
So I ain't frontin' …
he knows he got it comin'.
He knows the lifespan of a hater
but I'm gon' have to do dat later.
And my Granny don't be sayin' nothin' even when she's able
'cause she knows that my hustlin' puts food on the table.
Man, I gotta get my hustle on just so I stay alive.

I gotta get out and hustle
so my family can survive.

Check Yer 6!

Check your six! Check ... your ... six!
Uncle Sam is on a roll and he don't respect shit!
Three sixty-four and a wake up is my tour of duty.
I hump the boonies in the 'Nam but I ain't so sure that it suits me.
This war is politicized ... the conflict is propagandized.
The draft board arrested me without being properly Mirandized.
I had to buy the only thing the judge had for sale:
"Sign up for Vietnam or take my Black ass to jail."
A Black man gets played like a slave
in The Land of the Brave ...
The Home of the Free?!?
Man, this ain't my war! Why the fuck y'all need me?
Helmet strapped down tight ... my bayonet is affixed
but Charlie ain't my enemy ... Black man check your six!
Uh ... Pardon me, Sarge ... 'cuse me if I'm wrong
but I ain't heard the word "nigger" comin' from no damned Viet Cong.
As we chase Charlie into Laos and across Cambodia's borders
the Lt. keeps on sayin', "We're just following orders."
But Charlie ain't got no more than I do from I can see.
Man, this ain't my war! Why the fuck y'all need me?
Send us a fire mission 'cause Sarge is poppin' off smoke!
Locate us with them rounds and bring it in close!
Check yer fire! Check yer fire!
The enemy is here! We got zips in the wire!
Air Cav chopper is overhead ... the sixty gun blazing from the door.
We tag 'em all and bag 'em all as casualties of war.
The entire 23rd infantry division of NVA

is massacred and slaughtered with innocent villagers in My Lai
as the real enemy cheats death in this Triangle of Iron
'cause Uncle Sam never had to live in Harlem nor Saigon.
Uncle Sam never lived within a third world nation
and Uncle Sam never, ever learned to stop hating.
That's what I think and I might be wrong
but I ain't never been called "nigger" by no damned Viet Cong.
So, maybe the day might come when Uncle Sam will see
that this ain't my war, man ... why the fuck he need me?

2 Protect & Serve Who?!?

To protect and serve who?
And who can protect US from you?
All y'all seem to be serving US
is harassment and abuse.
Police brutality is our brutal reality.
To protect and serve?!?
Huh!!!
Respect US first.

Injustice Case

United?
Our states are not.
See how high the stakes have got?
Divided WE have fallen.
Ignoring the sound our nation's calling.
No one can argue that America the Beautiful's
ugly assed actions are despicably undisputable.
And even that lovely Liberty lady
is in cahoots and acting shady.
Sweet land of liberty?
What has this country given me?
Y'all can see what WE gave
o'er the land of the free and the home of the brave …
O say can *who* see what so proudly WE hail?!?
No … say can *you* see what WE loudly call Hell?
And good Ole Glory swaying in the breeze
seems a bit more gory paying reparations to the Japanese
while WE Black folk are still due
our 40 acres and a mule.
Just in case you didn't know
its an injustice case
that me and all of my people must face.
WE built this nation or carried the shit that built it
And WE thought of, discovered, or designed much of the shit WE get killed with
because our corrupt government acts empowered by impunity
and undue rights are to given them through diplomatic immunity.
See, United WE stand

and divided WE fall …

There is no liberty
but there's injustice …

There is injustice for all.

2nd Generation Son

I am a second generation son
American bred and born
carrying blood
from other nations
separated
long before my time
so, instead I embrace
and carry proudly
what you outwardly see
—this African skin.

My daughter is born
to the son of a son
of a son of the island.
So I endeavor
never
to allow
that bit of Hispanic within me now
to be lost or ignored
no more
than I have allowed her to ignore also being African.
Although
English is the only language I know,
how else will she know
from what little is shown
to African American
Children?

I speak broken Spanish
and few African words
except for the Swahili I have heard.
But if I do not show her
she may see
and she will not understand.
Then what kind of father
or man
would I be?
Pieces of me
have already been forgotten
before they were taught to me.
I am trying to retain
whatever remains
from the heritage within my name
and the blood coursing through my veins.
The blood of conquistadors and ocean explorers
and Zulu Kings and Ashanti warriors
and Alabama back roads
and Cleveland, Ohio
and Philadelphia streets
is all within the blood both our hearts beat.
And she needs to know this.

Raised the flag as I raised my fist and raised my socio-political consciousness from that of a mis-educated Negro. Vaingloriously; in honor of our fallen heroes like Black Americans making a covenant for the brothers and sisters struggling but barely making So unbearable at times WE barely are taking it. Disenfranchised from the American dream as a nightmarish reality birthed for US a militant mentality and as WE newfound mental militants hear the voices of resistance, WE make life long decisions in an instant. From a doctrine of separate but equal to proclaiming "Power to the People!" And ain't no small

proceed

HOPE

youth

promise

Inner City
Obsessions

Inner city obsessions
and questions to life long lessons
keeps me guessing at the impossible
and is perhaps undaunted yet improbable
like the burning down of the brick city
and "niggas hatin' but y'all cain't get with me".
So many lost souls bought and sold …
dead urban soldiers with stories untold
fading away like smoke from crack rock
haunting street corners, back alleys, and vacant lots.
No longer kings and queens …
no longer having dreams …
shattered like broken glass in brown bags,
scattered like thrown down trash.
Laid out in the gutter transparent and see through
are the songs of my inner city people
'cause I am them and they are me
with the same wants and needs from life lived differently.

2 Know Thy Self

He awaits the return or
for
the rise of some hero.
The mis-educated Negro.
He sleeps.
Moments … minutes … hours … weeks …
Lacking true knowledge of self,
he cannot help himself.
This descendent of the Danhomee,
not knowing
that the blood flowing through his veins
is the same
as their highly revered Panther Kings.
Unfamiliar with Divine Mother Yemanja.
Ignorant to the writings of Mawulisa.
Predestined.
His Fa is to be their heir.

CO-INTEL-PROSE
(Wack Patriot's Act)

COINTELPRO (Counter Intelligence Program) …
targeted against politically radical, left-winged elements …
charged with rounding up anarchists and revolutionaries …
conducted from 1956 to 1971.

No matter what was said,
the blood was shed as COINTELPRO
would show and tell so
J. Edgar Hoover's Federal Bureau of Investigation
could make good on their dedication
to domestic counter intelligence:
coercion of witnesses,
and drumming up evidence,
with break-ins,
illegal wiretaps,
and the opening of mail,
while bogus, trumped up charges had US going to jail
from covert surveillance by the police
based solely on our political beliefs.
They made their business
the harassment of "dissidents".
Played propaganda and
conducted political assassinations
and infiltrations
in order to disrupt,

discredit,
and misdirect.
See, our freedom to speak
and our freedom to associate
were Constitutional guarantees
that they would readily violate
all in the name of preserving American democracy.
There is hypocrisy that WE can surely see
in the term "Homeland Security".
So as patriots act,
WE must question one fact:
who is really the terrorist?

(Wasted American Resources)
WAR on Drugs

It was the so-called war on drugs
that labeled US as thugs.
Just a bunch of Blacks on crack
who sell,
who use,
or either abuse cocaine.
A dope game theory.
Y'all hear me?
Could have been seized easily
out of the air,
or in the waters.
Even confiscated at our borders.
But it was a dope game theory.
Y'all hear me?
Instead of posting indictments on foreigners,
they wait to raid inner city stash houses
and street corners.
No Columbians.
Not Bolivians
nor Peruvians.
With our politicians pardoning intrusions
of kilos
as briefcases of C Notes

move G Packs
that create stacks.
And as for corruption,
the real weapons of mass destruction
use mass production
and distribution
through well established markets
for some well established profits
as WE get well acquainted in jails or in coffins
with a dope game theory.
Y'all hear me?
Still WE won't indict drug cartels from the South America
nor corrupt U.S. corporations either
although to process cacao plants
into base cocaine you need ether
supplied by our American oil companies.
Something WE don't see
because its a dope game theory.
Y'all hear me?
Corrupt politicians got our votes
but US Black folks ain't got no planes or boats
so Blacks folks ain't the importers.
Start the war on drugs at our borders
and put an end to this dope game theory.
Do y'all hear me?

NIGGER

I might wear a uniform
or one piece cover-alls may be worn,
a black hoodie,
a throwback jersey,
tux and tails,
or Timbs and a white tee,
white shirt and tie,
or tie dyes,
African beads, a kufi, and dashiki,
or have on a cap and gown
with a diploma
and a degree
but some may see me
and only see
a nigger.
All shades of fine
can be found
from charcoal black to
cocoa brown,
from caramel cream,
to honey molasses,
from hazelnut toned,
to high yellow,
to red boned
my skin shades range from
but all are synonymous with nigger to some.
I span across wearing dreads

to bald heads,
and corn rows,
or afros,
with conks,
curls,
and cold waves
along the way
but all that some may see
is a nigger when they look at me.
I went from nigger
to negra
to negro
to colored folk,
Afro American,
Black American,
African American,
to nigga
and then
back to nigger again
'cause that is all that some are willing to see
when they look at me.

Civil war. Insurgency. Demonstrations of urgency. Same as civil unrest and protest. So, our whole world now becomes the Modern Babylon or perhaps just a poor excuse for US to drop the bomb. But WE got revolutionary ideas that aint so brand new. A circumference of 360. Ya dig me? Wearing the symbolism of anarchism, as anarchists arise and become recognized turning things around through revolution. We open our eyes. Oppose the Antichrist, and his final solution. Prophesized within the Book

Modern Babylon

The fault rests with the government
but is laid at the feet of the president.
It is written in The Book of Revelations
on the Apocalypse
as the evidence.
Iraq way back,
also known as Babylon,
when examined now
is seen the same as Vietnam.
Some of those same horrors
from Sodom and Gomorrah
to Saddam Hussein.
Its so damn insane.
And Bush
is getting US ambushed.
Civil war.
Insurgency.
Demonstrations of urgency.
Same as civil unrest and protest.
So, our whole world now becomes the Modern Babylon
or perhaps just a poor excuse
for US to drop the bomb.
But WE got revolutionary ideas that ain't so brand new.
A circumference of 360.
Y'dig me?
Wearing the symbolism of anarchism,
as anarchists arise

and become recognized
turning things around through revolution.
WE open our eyes,
oppose the Antichrist,
and foil his final solution.
Prophesized within the Book of Daniel.
Proven to be too much for him to handle.
Until he lies sword and shield down by the riverside
and studies war
no more.

1nce African Kings

WE were once African Kings.
Now we're street kings.
Living and losing lifetimes by gambling
or straight out scramblin'
on street corners and city blocks.
Constantly clocking the competition and cops
POP! POP! POP!
"Aw … shit! Thangs done got hot!"
But it seems like it gets a little too hot too often.
Only two exits out are in jail or in a coffin.
And all the while
as the young bodies pile
more bodies keep droppin'
Jacked up by the cops and
POP! POP! POP!
Some more bodies drop
as young thugs sell drugs
and settle their beef with slugs
that ends with a shovel but only started with a shove?!?
Kids pictures on T-shirts sayin': "R.I.P." or "1ne Love".
Young lives lost literally over chasing a dollar.
Sometimes it makes me want to holler!
'Cause its hard for me to see these things
and then to think that WE were once African Kings.

Inclusion makes equality. Oppression makes a fist. Truly oppressed people are a risk ... be quiet ... looting ... a corrupt police shooting ... civil disturbance used to remove our burden. Whether or not to rather be quiet? Do WE accept separate but equal or go with status quo? Well, why not just

Clenched Black Fists

Inclusion makes equality.
Oppression makes a fist.
Truly oppressed people take a risk ...

rioting ... looting ...
a corrupt police shooting ...
civil disturbance ...

used
to remove
our burden.

Whether to riot
or rather be quiet?

Do WE accept separate but equal
or go with status quo?

Well, why not
just boycott?

(A Mother's Pain)
WE Cain't Explain

WE cain't explain
a mother's pain.
As she grieves,
she receives our regrets
and she cries as the sun sets.
Her son died,
she yelled out ...
she cried.
With due sympathy,
heads bowed.
Curiosity seekers not allowed.
WE remain.
WE agonize.
WE feel the pain within her cries.
A deep pain that WE all share
in our thoughts
and in our prayers
because WE cain't explain a mother's pain.
Offering our condolences
and consoling
for the young life that was stolen.
One more mother robbed of her son
by someone else's child ...
by someone else's gun.
One child remains ...

one life left to pay the cost.
So two young lives have been lost.
As WE complain
that WE cain't explain,
those grim reminders of the mothers' grief …
her trials …
her cries of denial …
her feelings of disbelief.
Finding no relief for the families
grieving the loss of their brothers .
And WE pray
for those grieving mothers
but WE cain't ever explain.

Prison Psalm

I am imprisoned.
Condemned.
Trapped by my sins.
Of what I have done.
Of where I have been.
My heart longs
for days now gone.
Sadly singing along
melancholy melodies of my prison song.
Pondering all that I have done wrong.
Longing for home.
Imprisoned alone.
Accompanied only by the pain that I feel.
Held back not by steel,
or by cinder block, or by concrete
but by time
and by these thoughts in my mind.

Roots Y'all

I'm talkin' 'bout down south.
See, we rollin' on down Crenshaw y'all
but we ain't gon' be on The Boulevard
saying "Hey Thug?" or "What up Cuz?"
We ain't even gon' be playing them dozens
but my blood kin cousins gon' be playing by the dozens.
Down south—
Where its blood in and blood out
with some strong family bonds to maintain
but we don't gangbang.
Where the streets ain't paved with
broken glass vials.
Not in denial about the crack in the streets
but they're only cracks in the pavement.
Where the heaviest Chevy
sitting on some "thangs"
ain't a SS or an Impala but
an old, rusty blue Chevrolet pickup truck
sitting up on cinder blocks or "somethang".
Its been there for years.
We never could fix on it,
so we'd just sit on it.
I'm talkin' 'bout down south y'all—
With these high standards we got,
our drive-bys just wave hi
leaving no innocent bystanders shot.
Where we can lay back and relax calmly.

Not palm trees but a shade tree fades me
and there ain't nobody actin' shady.
Where the rib dinners ain't never been served in no Styrofoam box
like some down the way rib spot
but where kinfolk sit
down at the barbecue pit
to play, reminisce, and talk shit.
No traffic.
No stray bullets
No dope fiends.
No gaming nor schemes.
Like magic,
that's been washed away before our eyes
as we roll in
on down Crenshaw with crimson tides.
Where I can truly get a sense *who* I am.
Where a pound and "What's up fam?"
are replaced by the love
and the hugs
from family.
I'm talkin' 'bout down south—
The truth y'all?
Just talkin' 'bout my roots y'all.

Soul Sisters

Answers given
on our ancestors risen.
Resurrected.
Spoken lyrics
on the spirits of ancestors
to Black Panthers.
Harriet Tubman and Sojourner Truth.
Learning the burning truth about Angela Davis or
Assata Shakur.
Kathleen Cleaver.
Controlled whispers
for my soul sisters
who held things down for US brothers
because they loved US.
Called nigger,
niggress,
nigga,
or niggette
yet were Nubianesque queens.
Treated US brothers like kings.
Fed US our freedom
as they led US to freedom.
Stood right by our side and cried as Panthers partied.
'Til questions ended and answers started.
Our ancestors
were sisters who blessed US.
For the pathways paved,

homage is paid
for those that birthed
and nursed
and mothered the revolution.

Cracked Up

He got popped by a cop
but wasn't he also a cop?
Undercover and dirty,
y'heard me?
Dirty cops using pawn shops
as legitimate business fronts.
Is that what y'all want?
Murder,
extortion,
racketeering,
and drug dealing
hidden behind badges.
A thug gets revealed and
as for the might of the pen ...
the sword ...
the gavel ...
the gun ...?
I guess crime really does pay for some.
Our world is literally cracking up
but, somehow, WE must
back it up.

She's somebody's
"Daddy's little girl".
Sucking dicks
and turning tricks
and being used by the world.

Abused by the world.
And abused by herself.
Made slave to the crack pipe.
Bypassed the help and the love of her family.
Smokes her way into one calamity
after another …
after another.
Her children get raised by their grandmother
while she haunts 'hoods and blocks.
Hopping into any car that stops.
Another trick.
Another sequel
among the volumes of other used people.
Our world is literally cracking up
but, somehow, WE must
back it up.

And he couldn't hold out
as he sold out his mama's hopes and joys.
He chose to be a dope boy.
No high school diploma, so fuck a college degree!
He posts out on street corners
with no particular place to be.
Got glass vials filled with rocks
sold out of his socks
or stashed in the bus stop.
Holding down his block.
Hangs out with his boys and
peddles and pushes his poison.
Poisoning
some other mother's hopes and dreams.
Our world is literally cracking up
but, somehow, WE must
back it up.

They played him like a high priced fool.
All through high school
he was loved by them

because he played his game above the rim.
Took his team to the state championship.
He blew out his knee.
From that injury,
he ain't got shit.
Traded in the college scouts
for corner boys and pee-wee look-outs.
Moves weight by the keys.
Used to wait for the shot at the top of the key
or posted down low and passed the rock.
Now he posts low down
and passes the rock.
His true story
lies beyond the glory.
Not hardwood but hard knocks.
Our world is literally cracking up
but, somehow, WE must
back it up.

They used to be innocent children
playing outside of project buildings
as daddy dealt drugs out back
and mama smoked her crack.
With no mama or daddy to raise them,
granny stepped in and she tried to save them.
She gave all that she had and she didn't have much
except her home and her love
which should have been enough.
She sent them to school all week
and took them to church on Sundays.
Got on her knees at night and she prayed that one day
her grandbabies would have just one thing—
to grow up and become something.
She gave both children the same love
but one grew up to be a cop
while the other one sold drugs.
Our world is literally cracking up.

but, somehow, WE must
back it up.

So, arise Black Man!
Show your pride as you
make a stand! Rejoice
and praise your
Blackness! Taking your
raised Black fist and
using it to extend a
helping hand to
rebuild your

proceed
Movement
oppo
RESISTANCE

A Typical Negro

What is a *typical* negro …?!?

Atypical negro,
a type of nigga,
or a typical *nigga*?
Might be so:
Type A negro?
Exactly *what* is typical
and what can be
correctly put politically?
Or rather put politically correct?
Whether given to US live and direct
or beaten around the Bush
like the NAACP,
the Urban League,
or Operation PUSH
comes to shove
comes to push …
and WE new found militants
express a profound vigilance over ignorance
on the trials and tribulations of our Black nation.
Combating further exploitation
as a champion of causes
like Mike Tyson fought fights.
Same as Dr. Michael Eric Dyson fights for civil rights.
And ain't no mystery.
Just go back and reread the history

on how the Black Panther Party
and other underground liberation movements
brought US some much needed improvement for the 'hood.
Modeling Fort Hood's 761st Tank Battalion,
the original Black Panthers' motto:
"Come Out Fighting"
Read the writing.
See, the revolution was always being televised
but WE have been watching the wrong channels.
An age-old divide and conquer stratagem
proven too much for US to handle.
Always had the RED, the BLACK, and the GREEN
so WE already know exactly what it means!
Nowadays WE add the GOLD
for those vast amounts of riches they stole.
Last Poets said, "Niggas are scared of revolution."
But need I remind US who it is doing the shootin'?
Let US use very same energy
but channeled differently
to bring about a change.
For far too long have WE had too much of the same.
Malcolm X and Dr. King are gone.
May God rest their souls until WE all return home.
Because left to watch US are the children.
So, my brothers and sisters,
it is time WE start building
a renaissance with pride
in the spirits
and in remembrance
of those of US who fought and died.
Following the proclamation
of our emancipation,
WE had Black Codes
and Jim Crow was legitimized.
Supreme Court intervention gave rise
Followed by
the inherent unconstitutionalities
and the fallacy

in the Civil Rights Act of 1875,
came literacy tests
and poll tax
from shiftless and
sneaky assed pole cats
discounting and
disregarding understanding
backed with a novel called <u>The Clansman</u>
and a motion picture named "The Birth of a Nation"
further legitimizing racist legislation.
Peculiar?
Because it should sound familiar
when nowadays,
with a Congressional filibuster,
the whole show can be stopped by one monkey,
be it an elephant or a donkey,
whose only cause to be furthered benefits their own.
Called our president but he rules from a throne.
Yet not using our right to vote
is like refusing to fight these folks.
Bloodshed by ballots
as valid as bullets
with niggers on triggers
get ready to pull it.
But some of US negroes
will still call this *typical*.
And it is as problematic for US
in that it is so political.
Now back on to donkeys and elephants.
Need I speak more on the relevance?
Sometimes a donkey is just merely an ass
while an elephant can be a tool
to be used
to cross over a mountainous pass
conquering an empire
and vanquishing cannibals who live like animals
in the same warrior-like spirit
of the great leader Hannibal.

But nothing
whatsoever
like a *typical negro*.
So, arise Black Man!
Show your pride as you make a stand!
Rejoice and praise your Blackness!
Taking your raised Black fist
and using it to extend a helping hand
to rebuild your communities
and uplift your brother, man.

Critical Conditions

CRITICAL THOUGHT NOW!
CRITICAL THOUGHT NOW!
WE watched as crack cocaine
drained
the life and vitality
out of a community.
It was sad to see.
CRITICAL THOUGHT NOW!
WE
selfishly watched helplessly
as helplessness
turned into hopelessness.
Turned US to dealing dope and shit.
WE watched it grow
out of control
as if
it went renegade.
Played
like some cataclysmic systemic capitalists.
Why wonder
about world-wide hunger
despite trading oil for food?!?
In spite of competition from a "him or me" attitude?
CRITICAL THOUGHT NOW!
Calling for CRITICAL THOUGHT NOW!
First industrialization …
then globalization …

now domestication.
See, WE tore up some shit
then turned around and paid for it
but to the victor is supposed to go the spoils.
So, why do WE still pay a premium for Iraqi oil
with territorial authority
and an imposed sovereignty?
Cultural assimilation
being synonymous with
domestication.
And watching over US is supposed to be an American Eagle.
Supposed to mean free, although,
what does freedom mean
unless WE secure the blessings that freedom brings?
Estranged foreign relations
and domestic policy bothers me
but I ain't hatin'
on politicians politicin',
discussin',
debatin'
the decisions they are making
while taking way more off of the top.
Think naught?
I think not.
I call for CRITICAL THOUGHT NOW!
A call for protest
for US to go out
and to go get.
Employ terrorism
or heroism?
Revolution:
does it always mean revolting
or does it sometimes mean revolving?
Involving
WE who have the least to lose
but the most to prove.
Global warfare and conflict
fought by young and poor men

although it is old, rich men who started it.
Those in control and
planning.
In the background standing.
Pushing buttons.
Talking loud but saying nothing.
Inevitably a catastrophe.
But is that the way that it has to be?
CRITICAL THOUGHT!
Caught
up in the system
without wisdom
and without knowledge sought.
Yet pathway seeking.
Researching
and reaching
and questing
while questioning.
Asking for
CRITICAL
THOUGHT
NOW!

WE idly waste our precious time. WE refuse to learn from our mistakes and to see the point so WE keep spending our best years inside the joint or WE waste our precious time away on street corners and WE spend our money with foreigners. WE have been physically freed while WE remain in a state of slavery into is a slavery of the mind. It is something that WE have lost and for some reason WE are unable to find. But some say, if you free your mind then your ass will follow. So, WE need to be spending our precious time like

WISDOM

knowledge

proceed

CRITICAL THOUGHT

Bad Politics

Bad politics gives US,
founding fathers who told lies,
who stole lives,
and who silenced those of US whom dared to ask why.
But small wonder
why bad politics gave US,
more pieces in a bigger puzzle to ponder.
Back in the 1700's,
shiploads of Africans made Americans
by landing in Annapolis, Maryland.
Human chattel as stock
stood atop of an auctioneer's block
then sold into slavery like cattle.
Bad politics gives US,
a doctrine of equality despite separation
that means little without overdue reparations
to level the playing field.
Bad politics gives US,
prophets who'll fight ghetto poverty
citing ghetto sovereignty
while netting profits from bribery,
fraud and illegal kickbacks,
swindles or evasion of tax,
with imminent domain,
or embezzlement
resulting from cataclysmic capitalists
in cahoots with the government.

Bad politics breeched
our Constitutional guarantees to freely speak.
But our rights ordained
so verbal expression remains inalienable.
Breeding social commentary
as political attacks.
Speaking out on the war in Iraq.
not unlike the one
that was fought in Vietnam;
a proven undoing for Black families.
Synonymous with calamity.
Synonymous with holocaust.
Synonymous with atrocity.
Synonymous with bad politics.
While domestic wars wage over police states,
with rage WE discuss and WE debate.
Do the cops truly "protect and serve"
or do they just "patrol and control" our communities?
Never being indicted by grand juries
because they inquest themselves
and then acquit themselves of any wrongdoing.
Permitting long periods
and histories of brutality
and abuses ensuing
with the blood of our martyrs
flowing like the reddest rivers of troubled waters
through our communities.
These bad politics
would seem to commit
political suicide.
Critical.
Like do or die.
Mamas cried
as justifiable homicides
became legalized lynching.
And playing propaganda
brought both the rise
and the demise of the Panther

and pimped the martyrdom
of Brothers Martin and Malcolm
but now has the Panther lying dormant.
Voices silenced
by the singing of paid informants
and bad politics
as democracy gets
redefined by our government's
arrogance.
Or is it ignorance?
Dismissing the will of the People.
Disenfranchising folks.
Miscounting votes
using nothing less than bad politics.

A Bonified
(Black Man, Money
Green)
Hustler

Rather be known as a bonified hustler
or a bonified struggler?
Peep game, my brother.
Recognize—
A perception
held onto long enough becomes a belief.
A belief held onto strong enough
becomes reality.
With little
or no proof,
perception and belief become truth
strong enough to shed blood
and crumble kingdoms
in search of freedom.
As the hypocrisy of democracy says:
"All men are created equal",
it speaks so keen
but what does equality mean
if you are not a free, white man
that owns land?
See, democracy

is inexplicably
bound to education.
But do WE
need to be
well trained or well educated?
As WE discussed and debated,
they brainwashed US into believing
that acting Black
is also acting ignorant.
Or being Black and being strong
is thought to be too militant.
As WE speak with a unified voice,
choice involves change
because change involves choice.
Choose which threat is greater:
a Black man with something to prove
or one with nothing to loose?
And as for this pride in our African heritage—
they're scared of it.
But their reasons are unclear.
Their motives are unseen.
After all, they may see a Black Man
but ain't his money green?
Just another bonified brother for the struggle
out here getting paid for his troubles.

It's All Smoke (& Mirrors)

The political smoke and mirrors
causes them to fail to hear US.
It has US yearning.
Taking issue over flag burning
or the rights so-called fags are earning.
They try to scare US
with talk against gays and same sex marriage.
A broken system
called capitalism.
Capitalizing off our fears.
Using political smoke and mirrors,
US citizens
get it again.
Figuratively and literally,
they've smoked up the mirrors politically.
They'd rather incarcerate—
use locked bars and gates
rather than to educate.
Our president George Bush
gives US residents a large push
and as push comes to shove,
WE no longer show love.
WE close our borders to illegal immigrants
like the smoke used to hide the guilt in mirrors showing innocence.
WE arrive at this derivative

as the cost of education becomes cost prohibitive.
Another example of supply-side demand being market driven
with profits risen along with tuition
and the powers that be
are getting rich by not listening.
Its as American as racism and apple pie,
that he who fails to see the hate in him
can never grapple with "why?"
So, he won't take a look in the mirror long enough to see it
and he will never
clear away enough of the smoke
for him to be it.

Media, Myself, & I

In the so-called same game ...
On the so-called same page ...
Talking a good game
of so-called revolution.
But WE will continue watching different channels
and not find our revolution being televised
unless WE all channel the same energy
differently
as one people
with one struggle.

Media,
myself, and I.
WE rely on the word of the street ...
on what is heard on the street
by he who ignores US
or whom fears US.
Failing to hear US.
America has no reasons to lie
but she lies for no reason
and those lies WE keep believing.
False media confronted
with a quest called knowledge:
a revolutionary movement.
Theorized and proven.
Combating fucked up false media.
Revolution now televised.

Set to channel zero as WE watch it.
See Black on Black violence but fail to stop it.
Driven by false media.
Given same faults.
Outdated as encyclopedias.
Like Black Ops or COINTEL
WE don't ask.
They don't tell
that legislative, judicial, and executive
viewed in the proper perspective
leaves our government exposed
as a government controlled
system of checks and balances.
Not three branched and triangular
but shaped pentagonal
with our military and media flanked on the diagonals
of an outdated, Americanized democracy.
Fed by the hypocrisy of our mutated system
of cataclysmic capitalism.
A sort of fascism keeps separate
the haves and the have nots
from those who have more
or those who ain't got
through false media
controlled by the right-wing.
Wag the dog
on the tail end of unpopularized fighting
an over propagandized war
as the rich get more
while the poor remain poor.
And WE get greedier
due to false media
via newspapers,
podcasts,
internet blogs,
and television broadcasts.
With media, myself, and I
left to wonder and

questioning why?
False media
WE don't need it do WE?

(Guerrillas) In the Midst

In the midst of the city,
a child cries.
Such a pity that no one hears him.
The child within soon dies so people fear him.
Fearful that they may also see his pain.
In time, only ghosts
and their echoes remain
in the midst of the city.

Str8 Gangsterism

Real gangsters
cain't just choose between
him or me
or them
or WE.
The M.O.B.—men of business
take care of business as
witnesses
and snitches are made to disappear
before anyone lends an ear.
Left to the gangsters like a federal cover up;
nothing less than corrupt.
Just like one bad apple left in a bushel
spoils the whole bunch
the same as a Bush will.
Not unlike a presidential pardon,
the political influence
makes US mad at you constituents
as attitudes harden
for a small but powerful man who sits in a White House.
Through the eye of the storm
WE search for a lighthouse to shine its beacon.
Poor and disenfranchised folks reaching
for an American Dream.
Hearing US scream
for a dream deferred
or a dream denied.

Some of US cried
as some of US awakened to a living nightmare.
Sent over to foreign lands for US to fight there
with all of the domestic problems at home
ignored or left alone.
Straight gangsters
with plenty of blood money made
and plenty of hush money paid.
Nothing more than a gangster
as the leader of a nation.
True taxation without representation
is nothing more than just another executive decision.
As WE assume the position,
the presumption of guilt
is assumed over innocence.
Presumed for only one reason—
no one dares to call it treason.
Like taking two to the head.
Cement shoes for the dead.
And our thing is more gangster
than La Cosa Nostra.
Braving mass media exposure
while playing tricks
and preaching politics
on an unholy, unjust war
but their organized crime
only shortens our time.
Gangsters same as good fellows
while those "good ole boys"
shake hands and say hello.
Corrupt politicians in cahoots
with crooks in big business.
No surprise—
the term derived
is known as a gangster capitalist.
Corporate board of directors
got a senator in the pocket
so laws cannot stop it.

From corporate bail-outs
to congressional sell-outs,
an entire nation
can be ruined through legislation.
As the facts state,
the richest 1% receive tax breaks
and Iraq escape.
More privileges
for those who are already privileged.
But the underprivileged and poor
get shuttled off to war
by a government backed gangster.
Like mob hits,
political ties to big business nets profits.
With my people on the outs
peeping through the keyhole.
Our government is more gangster than Al Capone
or Bugsy Siegel.
Like Meyer Lanski
it seems that our politics can be
straight gangster.
WE remember that: "Some gave all ... all gave some".
Just like Vietnam
yet WE fail to remember those who now fall.
Discounted by some in Iraq
and by others, not counted at all.
Crooks get caught
but with amnesty for those who paid more.
Bought and paid for legislation
as rip-offs,
and pay-offs,
and kick backs
net back big stacks
of large, untraceable bills
from under-the-table deals
written in the blood of American soldiers
daring the exposure from the false media conglomerates
also government controlled;

censoring all too often
the flag draped coffins
with our casualties of war
casually written off as a loss
along with the corporate tax write-offs
and the tax breaks for the wealthy.
Denying that its gangsterism but WE will see
who is guilty.

WE Shall Overcome

The young folks don't know what our race has done
because they don't know where we've come from.
No one has told them that RED, BLACK, and GREEN stands
for our blood ... our race ... our Motherland.
Like they say that "a mind is a terrible thing to waste",
time is a terrible thing to wait
but our government has made no preparations
to get US our overdue reparations.
"It wasn't me ... my grandfather owned slaves"
ignoring the wealth and riches that their grandfather gave
that were stolen from our legacy
is something that was said to me.
"But slavery happened so long ago",
while paying no restitution for resources that they stole.
And while there is no statute of limitations on murder,
our calls for reparations continue to go unheard of.
Black folks who don't agree that reparations are fair
need merely keep quiet and relinquish their share.
Special Field Orders No. 15 would have set precedent,
but it was vetoed and betrayed by Andrew Johnson as president.
Unsympathetic and flat out racist.
Denied US due compensation while giving no basis.
WE gave them folks no reason to hate US.
WE got no mule and no 40 acres.
So, preparations need to be made
and reparations need to be paid
for our bottled up aggression

due to over 400 years of oppression.
And finally, WE SHALL OVERCOME!
As, my light shines bright like the sun
with skin as dark as an eclipse
because it was my gift
that was delivered by slave ship.

A Mis-education
(neo-Blaxploitation)

Nowadays
there is a neo-Blaxploitation
going on in this nation.
The conservatism that it preaches
never teaches
that Black culture is so much deeper
than soul food or Ebonics;
not just some language that WE speak
nor the food that WE eat.
But like a modern day slavery,
its all a big part of this right-winged plot
to keep US from closing the gaps
between the haves
and those who have not.
A mis-education
from amiss education
provides a missed education
but its all common knowledge.
Definitive of truth acquired following graduation from college
but sort of oxymoronic in terms
as WE learn
that if knowledge were truly common
then WE would all have it.
Spoken on first
and left with after thought as the tactic.

With a militancy preached that may seem fanatical.
An overwhelming response
because the federal government is responsible
for the pain and the plight
of Black folks' struggle and strife
and our diminished quality of life
and the quantity of lies on the exploitation
and now on this neo-Blaxploitation.
Just one more crisis within our nation.

A Quest Called Knowledge: The People's Movement

The all seeing third eye shines
illuminating pilgrimages made during past times.
Peering eastwardly,
enabled to see clearly back to Mecca
as if looking through the eye of Amun Ra,
WE behold a perfect view of The Supreme Being
given to US for naught more than believing.
Our time has come once again.
If WE truly seek to emerge from the darkness,
WE must heed the words that our elders have harkened
and find the knowledge within the light that WE seek.
It calls US to arise, my brothers and sisters, and proceed to the east.

Public Enemies?!?

Some of US believe that they're all hood rich and rolling with 22's.
Thinking that they'll come for you;
not on B.F. Goodrich
but with Smith and Wesson as their choice of weapon.
See, America's public enemy is not Flav and Chuck D from PE.
America calls young Black males her public enemy.
Young brothers faced with their only choices left
to find their demise in jails, institutions, or death.
Because America sold it to them and they bought up
but then they try to sell it but they get caught up.
Young Black males get blackmailed with jail,
and blacklisted with bail.
They get black balled by hope,
black labeled with dope,
blacked out by intoxication,
and then blackmailed trying to avoid incarceration.
They get lost and confused and
chasing grandiose illusions
alluding to a video lifestyle that is o so surreal.
Oh?
So, who keeps it real
while my young brothers are caught up in all of the hoopla
and hype
of Hip Hop's hypocrisy
and financing America's materialistic, capitalistic democracy
through multi media marketing
and something called *bling bling*?

As text messages and cell phones ring
they sound the alarm that the revolution is now being televised on MTV.
The revolution is being televised and it is on BET.
Just watch channel zero to view the revolution
and see that all my young brothers ain't out there burnin', shootin', and lootin'
wearing ski masks with gats and claiming to be down.
Some young brothers with diplomas, degrees, and caps, and gowns
are coming soon to a neighborhood near you!
But they'll come rolling urban assault vehicles that sit low on 22's
with chrome Spreewell's a-spinnin', or Mo Mo's, or True's.
Although some may put on Kevlar vests just so they can rest
other young brothers may choose not to pick up those guns.
As public enemies prove that sometimes uzis do weigh tons
but they ain't so heavy
and neither is a young brother.
yeeaaah boy-eee!!!

By Any Means (& I Do Mean Any)

I got played,
prostituted,
and pimped
in an attempt to discredit me.
Should I just let it be?
Knowing that through hostility
and aggression
WE bring about an end to that oppression.

By any means, and I do mean any …
Out of one comes many.
e plurbis unim
So, WE take it straight to them
as WE boycott to control our dollars spent
and WE hold demonstrations opposing the government.
As some of US riot,
WE refuse substandard service …
inferior goods—WE don't buy it.
WE come out and WE protest against all of the crack smoked.
Far as the eye can see there's Black folk.
One million and one raised Black fist
making up for lost time and days missed.
Our long awaited answers to the Final Call
because injustice for some ain't "justice for all".

He Would Be King

Now that WE own more capital,
would WE still march on our own Capitol?
Would WE still picket
and protest
and sit-in?
Or would WE sit down
or get let down
or go fetch just to get in?
See, WE used to boycott
avoid shots
from crooked cops
be debased by bigots
braved lynch mobs
police dogs
fire hoses
and billy-clubs
fat, cracker-assed sheriffs' cells
in southern county jails
and hick town racist mayors.
WE faced off against those racists' stares
back in the day.
But as for this day,
would "injustice anywhere"
still be "a threat to justice everywhere"?
Or would injustice ignored empower their oppression
until time triggered a Black-fisted aggression?
In these days of convenience

and expedience
would he still advocate for civil disobedience?
Had he not been silenced
would he still be preaching about nonviolence?
And for whom the Liberty Bell tolls
with our government in control,
would WE still just "let freedom ring"?
Yes, I am wondering
would he
still be
King?

Caught Between Iraq
& a Hard Place

Comin' straight forward
and headed straight for it
while most Republicans are beatin' around the bush.
WE need to be beatin' down on George Bush
if he steps out in the streets
making a speech.
Just like our founding fathers and descendents
made a Declaration of Independence
on the 4th of July,
it has caused you lie to US.
Young folks sent over Iraq to die for US.
Talkin' 'bout some "divinization".
A so called "divine making of a nation"
with no regard for lineage
or prayer
or complexion.
Our situation is vexing.
Caught between Iraq and a hard place.
A hard case can be made
that George and Dick and Condoleeza
make for damn sure I can't afford no condo lease or
house note or
apartment rent.
They made for damn sure that my money got spent.
But what the fuck was their plan?

Invade Afghanistan,
Iraq,
and then Iran?
The ancient Babylonians,
Mesopotamians,
the Sumerians,
and the Persians
same people—same place; just a different version.
WE got Uncle Sam over there hatin'
and them calling US the "Great Satan"
From the Shah
to the Ayatollah,
they want to take the west and put on a muzzle.
Got all of the pieces in a Persian puzzle
on the brink of a nuclear over-boil.
A potentially apocalyptic nuclear warfare over oil?!?
See, like our lies, they have fables
where coffins are more favorable than cradles.
Two choices left.
One choice is freedom.
The other choice is death.
Fuck what WE are talking about
because they embrace the freedom of death and go all out
with the scariest
use of insurgents, guerillas, and terrorists.
Their homeland overflowing like fountain waters
with the blood of their martyrs.
As WE got caught between Iraq and a hard place,
the hard case could be made
for how US pawns in the game get played.

Wind, Water, & Horror

Wind,
water,
and horror.
An aftermath of devastation,
rubble,
and trouble
with most of the trouble brewing
amidst the rubble and the ruins
of New Orleans awaiting
the response of a nation.
Its ironic that the same means used to save me
had been employed during slavery.
With our families disgraced
and our families displaced.
Sent hither,
to and fro.
Our neighborhoods scattered to and fro.
Like our villages got scattered.
To and fro.
Meanwhile, WE strived to survive
or were WE just "looting"?
The National Guard wasn't prepared to save US
but they came prepared to do some shooting.
Its more than just embarrassing
because they were ignorant and uncaring

that a true refugee
has no country
but the media didn't see US as American citizens.
So were WE refugees
or were WE victims?
These ugly faces of racism
with US afraid of facing them
breeds a hatred that runs deep.
Like still waters.
Flood waters.

So Many Sons

So many sons know the pain that I feel.
My father's love denied me by hard prison steel.
The warmth his heart and hands held behind cold concrete.
Devoid of his presence by day and as I sleep.
Devoid of his wisdom and his embrace.
Devoid of his words and the vision of his face.
A strong man but there was more strength
in cinder block walls and metal chains
and my own imprisonment lies inside of my pain.

Prior Addictions

From crackheads
with wrapped heads
to weed heads
who wear dreds,
The Most High
hears most cries
from those most high.
With the most joyful highs
followed by
the most woeful lows.
Its truth exposed.
To induce joy
and kill the pain,
but then feel the same.
To provide an escape.
Or lay wide awake.
And for a short time life gets better
but then it gets heavier.
Bearing the weight of the world;
the burdens of earth.
Sent on a life-long search
but never finding what WE seek
makes strong men weak.
An addiction.
Like verbalized poeticism.
Vocalized diction.
Like hitting jackpots

off crack rocks
at crack spots.
And yeyo?
Just say "no"?
Or no say so?
Like lyrical dope fiends
who get high off of puffing
purple haze into smoke screens.
A gross error in judgment.
Dare not to say it wasn't
but who drinks
and then thinks logically?
No matter the habit,
'cause alcoholics
are also drug addicts.
Serving a life-long conviction
known as an addiction.
From bloodshot eyes
the tears cry
as fears rise
to epidemic proportions.
Increasing the cautions.
Sends them shooting up.
Like choices to get high:
huffing,
puffing,
popping,
piping,
snorting,
shooting up.
Poisons injected intravenously
provide verbal perspectives
given extemporaneously.
And once addicted,
always addicted.
Convicted.
Pled guilty for a victimless crime?
Read guilt-free from a rhythmless rhyme.

Evident in the evidence
and plain to see.
Blamelessly?
Victimless?
Or are there victims?
Witnesses of illicit miseries
and memories cooked up
in spoons or in cups
strained with cotton from cigarette butts
then sucked
up into our needles
keeps US peepin' through keyholes
trying to refill holes
in our hearts
and in our souls
but with a dope's game.

Another Hero 4 Hire

WE don't need another hero
just to marvel US
with his claims of being marvelous
while subtracting from zero in truth.
Claiming to fight for truth …
justice;
just US
and our American way.
Sometimes fighting the gays.
At other times he fights the guys
with shaved heads
or in white hoods.
But he also opposes brothers and sisters
infiltrating in white 'hoods.
Opposes US integrating.
Naw, WE don't need another hero.
What WE need is a revolution.
Not shooting.
Not tearing down.
But turning around
because WE had our own hero.
A Black Panther?
Well kind of—
He liked to chill like T'Challa,
King of Wakanda.
But to tame his rage,
WE locked him away in a cage.

Then bought US a hero for hire.
But WE don't need no other hero
as sell out negroes
and jealous niggas conspire.
Released from his cage
turned one more colorful page.
Read the words up in the bubble.
Put all the evil doers in trouble
as a Black Panther saves the day.
Like our predecessors who paved the way.
Like Fred Hampton.
Like George Jackson.
Like Huey P. Newton.
So WE sing that same hymn about a revolution
stolen from their history books
and comic books
by some kind of crooks.

Faces of Death

The wages of sin?
Death
with war being waged on whatever is left.
Fuck the glory
but its all guts and gory at times.
Its been said that Grand Theft Oil is the crime committed.
Although bullshitted on CNN broadcasts
and put off way past the deadlines,
WE can still read in the headlines of the Washington Post,
the LA Times, and newspapers from coast to coast.
But why can't WE all see this?
WE suffer the same injustices
from Sarajevo
to Soweto
to Somalia
or Bosnia.
Played by too much of the same.
Game theories
on the Israeli realities
of lobbing bombs into Lebanon,
Libya,
or Syria.
The same realities of Palestinian insurgents
as extremist splinter cells emerge and
become secretly shrouded
like suicide bombers when buses become crowded.
Hearing explosives cry

like hearing explosive cries.
Seen the same as through a soldier's eyes
the heinous crimes and atrocities.
Ferociously slaughtering innocents;
women and children.
Civilians
facing their deaths.
WE see their faces of death
replacing what is left
of our world as a stage
for senseless wars being waged.

Divided WE Fall

Those legacies
of slavery,
both unforgiving
and unforgiven,
carry US the mental message
of the middle passage—
a sort of natural aggression
based upon the theory of natural selection
where only the strongest survive.
It was dog eat dog in the hold of the slave ship to stay alive.
Survival of the fittest then figured
turn field slaves against house niggers.
Despite the emancipation of the negro type
instead of building nations acting hero-like.
Head plantation negroes now CEOs.
Black corporate head figures
same as big Black buck niggers.
Our 'hoods divided across colors.
Divided between brothers.
Where WE call home.
Killing and dying over what WE don't own
until WE see an urban exodus
simultaneous gentrification caused by a suburban influx.
Facing racism and classism.
A covert albeit systemized fascism.
Those culturally diverse population figures
of Jiggaboos, Bamas, Wannabes, and Wiggers

somehow causes US to fuss.
Somehow divides and conquers US.
Somehow keeps US on different pages.
Somehow keeps US sitting in cages.
Somehow keeps US from progressing.
Keeps US from addressing divisive issues.
Devastates our communities like nuclear missiles.
Leaving US barren and destitute
with those legacies of slavery as the cause at the root.

Classism

All WE want is a safe place to sleep
and something to eat,
but they lock the doors on their limos
and they ride by
peering out of the windows.
Leaving US with no sympathy.
Left the orchestra
or the symphony
having a night out on the town
in their full-length evening gowns
and After Six tuxedoes.
Giving a fuck less where WE go.
Got all dressed up
then stepped out
complacently
stepping past US in our transparency
as some of US lie down
outside in city parks.
WE sleep where it is cold,
vulnerable,
and dark.
Revealing
America's Dream
as nightmares.
Revealing
the ugliest faces of fascism
and classism.

Facing off our
aggressive pan-handlin'
harassing them
is seen as something more than rude.
"Will Work for Food"
but the sign says so much more.
Like a silent war
imposed by the wealthy
on those of US in poverty
as they walk past in disgust.
Literally stepping over US.
Saying things like "those people"
shows US how WE ain't equal.
Fed by the false media
filled with news
of sensationalist views.
Donning cashmere
at cash bars;
downing champagne
and dining on caviar.
While WE stand on the outs,
some of US shout, "Power to The People!"
because WE can get down too
and WE, The People, are getting restless
awaiting our name
to appear on some guest list.

His Honor

Jurors despised him.
His lawyer denied him help
and he denied himself of his honor.
His judgment was passed out by His Honor.
He sat there amazed in astonishment;
sentenced to death as capital punishment.
Paying back with his life
for the life that he robbed.
So, two lives were robbed
as well as both families left behind.
All victims of Black on Black crime.
Choosing not to speak,
he'll forever hold his peace
until arriving on Death Row
in the Belly of the Beast.
Only his last words will be heard.
Achieved only grief for both families.
Chose his life.
Paid the price.
He knows that he is a dead man walking
so he doesn't bother with talking.
Doesn't bother with confessing.
He won't start second guessing his choices and violence
or the voices that he has silenced.
Not just a husband and father's,
but the voices of widowed wives' and orphaned daughters'.
Silenced because

he was robbed of what he was
and robbed of what he would be.
Denied of what he could be.
True for both victim and assailant.
True for a system that keeps failing
because man can't judge man;
Only God can.

Aw Shucks!

Nigga, go 'head an' try tah white wash
yo' Black face …
dis Black race.
Cakin' on s'much ov dat white make up
dat you just luvs so much
but still performin' in black-face.
Y'still performs in disguise an' disgrace.
Keep on smilin' fo' massah.
Keep hidin' from the masses
and pretendin' tah be sumthin' you ain't.
Tryin' tah get intah sumwheres dat you cain't.
Keep on buckin'.
Keep on grinnin'.
Nigga, keep on tryin' tah fit in!
Nah sir.
Not me.
I sees dat wut is likely
is also likely so
fo' all those
sell-out,
Uncle Tom,
house negroes.
Gets tah dancin'!
Gets tah sangin'!
Gets tah doing so'mo' ov dat en-tah-tainin'!
Just a-shuckin' …
an' a-jivin' …

just tah stay alive an'
y'all stepin' fetchit,
sell-out niggas will continyah tah catch it.

Terrorist Who?!?

Do WE make the case for reparations
using due diligence
or just do
diddly?
Riddle me
and ask, "reparations how?"
as WE call for reparations now
because our just dues
are past due.
Terrorist who?!?

When little girls got killed in church bombings
but Black Baptist ministers only wanted to quiet and calm things.
Like our brothers getting shot down
in the back of alley ways
or in dark hallways
always unarmed
by rogue police who claim to have been threatened
yet appearing unharmed.
Who is the terrorist?!?

With mass media outlets
controlled by the Zionist
in London,
D.C.,
and Tel Aviv
deciding what WE see.

Broadcasting
government sanctioned
censorship.
Who is the terrorist?!?

As WE pay more for our gas
but with less money;
a redistribution of wealth
that somehow
only some see.
Peep the game
and you will see the same:
Iraq is Vietnam.
As heads of state nod in indecision,
Tel Aviv
tells no tales
on television.
Terrorist who?!?

WE made decisions
to over-flood the prisons.
By doing crimes,
WE do time,
lose time,
and lose minds.
The cells in jails packed
with Latinos and Blacks
disproportionately
as if it ought to be.
Denied civil rights.
After receiving the third strike,
put down for double life.
If reincarnated,
then re-incarcerated.
Who is the terrorist?!?

Leaving so many children behind
by *No Child Left Behind*

telling US how and who to educate
through its unfunded mandates,
a bad precedent is set
by a bad president
who plays with lives
by playing with lies.
Terrorist who?!?

Like dope dealers
and drug addicts
bringing ghetto dramatics,
WE have politicians on the take
and the laws that they make
support the special interests
of big business
while crooked cops
are pimping players
and playing pimps
at the neighborhood's expense.
So the People must pay;
both predators and prey.
WE got some of US just trying to pray
as others keep
walking around asleep.
Who is the terrorist?!?

With the will of the conservative moral majority
being imposed on US minorities,
some Christian fundamentalist fights
are no different than Muslim extremists like
Hamas,
al-Qaeda,
Mujahideen,
or Hezbollah.
While our Right-wing
is so out of touch that they don't know what is happening.
Labeling folks liberal;
like it's a bad thing.

Terrorist who?!?

WE radical folks
who may seem fanatical
about being outspoken
but with no laws broken?
Freedom of speech?!?
Freedom to assemble?!?
Freedom or death
through protests that resemble
demonstrations and boycotts
against those who have more
exploiting those of US who ain't got.
Terrorist who?!?

Like those urban myths WE don't believe in
about stores owned by Jews, Arabs, and Koreans
providing the drug dealers and hoodlums
supplies that promote violence and shootings.
Corner stores front the re-ups
along with quarter pops and Reesie cups
for teen-agers out on the block
as well as 30-somethings
as eyewitnesses see nothing
but say they might have heard of something.
The smugglers,
the hustlers,
even the customers.
Who is the terrorist?!?

After Math

In the aftermath, she dropped out of high school.
WE thought her to be a fool
but she has proved to be a mathematical genius.
She has seen just how many times
16 can go into 9
leaving a remainder of one.
Her calculations get done
although for that caper
she don't need no scrap paper.
She remembers to carry her ones
like she remembers to carry her guns.
Fanatical
about her mathematical abilities.
Inherent as she counts karats …
counts cabbage …
counts cheese.
To her a 9mm Glock
is a forget-me-not.
No doubt about it;
she don't leave home without it.
Her sexy looks ain't why this hottie is bangin'.
Don't call her a "whore"
'cause when she kicks in doors
her sawed off shorty leaves them hangin'!
Calculating.
Does her business mathematically.
Semi-automatically

slips in a clip.
Rata-tat-tat!
She got a gat
and fantastically
runs numbers
and runs guns
and runs hustles.
She runs the streets.
Provides the muscle.
Divides a brick into ounces
and then bounces
to get her block tight
and get her money right.
Clocking major figures
by subtracting
off fractions
from minor niggas
and just doing her math.

Fucked Up By US

A crime committed by Blacks against Blacks.
With one foot in the system and "The Man's" foot on our backs,
we spend penitentiary time
for Black on Black crime.
Divided but conquering nothing.
The state of our union is troubling.
Our bleak outlook on reality
comes from having a "nigga-tive" mentality.
Somehow thinking WE can be fed
off of nothing but "street cred"
with a Negro-like mindset.
How far can WE get?
To defy all of those stats,
those facts,
and those figures,
WE need to stop acting like typical niggas.
My brothers and sisters, WE need to free our minds and elevate.
WE need to achieve
and uplift
or there'll be hell to pay!

Bad Ass Mission
Aborted

WE cannot count how many
of our bad memories
got twisted into contortions
like breeched fetuses before abortions.
Brought forth through our revelations on revolution
with instinctive, adapted behaviors due to our evolution
as prisoners of a war on drugs—
a war on thugs
but the "war-zone" was where WE called home.
From anarchists to Anti-Christ,
the last vision that WE see
is a burning Bush in effigy.
Failed by him but it is WE who sit presidents.
Have WE set precedence
by coincidence
or as evidence?
Like the impunity for corrupt law enforcement.
But with broken laws
comes cause for atonement.
Yet WE only get tormented
and tortured by these
abandoned memories
until WE have truly set them free.
When no longer spoken of through lyrics
are the lost spirits of aborted fetuses

who eat at US.
No longer causing US cramping and pains
in our abdomen
as "The Man" kept US crouched down
in those fetal positions
which was reminiscent
of being chained in the dark filthy holds of slave ships.
Broken free from the grasps of mind-altering substitutions.
Broken free from bonds of enslaving institutions.
Freed of pent up resentment
and latent frustrations
caused by our waiting.
Free.
Finally, free.

African American't

American't
just emasculate fathers,
and rape mothers,
denigrate sisters,
and incarcerate brothers
by lying, stealing, and cheating.
But WE keep repeating the same thing—
doing insane things.
Scandalous like Watergate and Enron.
Scandalous like Iraq or Vietnam.
WE could be convicted every time.
Guilty of every crime.
Tempting fate
and attempting faith
through exploration
and exploitation.
While debating everything
from the Heavens
to the Holy Land,
Isaac to Ishmael,
and our Lord Jesus
to Jihad.
WE heard "YEE-HAA!" yelled
by bigots backed behind Confederate flags.
Dealt with inconsiderate fags
who placed their state of being above all else,
while the Black Man in America

lacked knowledge of self.
Permitting their likening of the gay rights movement
to the civil rights movement
as Uncle Sam sent the soul
over to Seoul—
a stop on the way over to Saigon
before days and long goodbyes gone.
Sent on our way
to die near the City of Hue—
or some other final destination in Southeast Asia.
But all America got was amnesia.
Once again WE fight for a nation
who never neither wanted
nor needed US to be there.
So, why care?!?
WE didn't back in 1968
but it was too late for US to get offended
until after the Vietnamese Tet Offensive.
WE rioted against the police in Chicago at the DNC,
but failed to protect Dr. King and Robert Kennedy
as LBJ declined the nomination for presidency.
O say could WE see
as African American't so proudly hails
many of our innovative Black minds
locked away inside America's prisons and jails?
African't American do what?!?
She does nothing but screws up!
WE got House Republicans' representation
accused of internet child molestation.
A full fledged investigation?!?
Or a full fledged cover up?
Bullshit so thick it nearly smothers US.
See, politics ain't nothing but hustle and flow.
A pimp game put on show.
As cowards,
and turn-coats,
and sell-outs
would burn most

as burn-outs would yell out.
Calling for "justice!"
But for just US
there was just this:
Emmett Till and Nat Turner,
LA, Detroit, and Chicago all burned up.
Like Cincinnati's riots,
the massacre at Rosewood was kept quiet
as was that incident in Tulsa
until explosive
time-bombs
find some
although laid to rest
and played their best.
As southerners slaved
in factories,
or out in fields,
or digging down in mines,
or working in mills.
Traversed trans-Atlantically
then traded coast to coast throughout a nation.
Prohibited US an education
with US kept separate but equal.
Status quo
as de facto segregation became the sequel,
increased the disparity between our people;
between the haves and have-nots.
Criticized by those that grab
as "those that grab naught",
or as "shiftless and lazy"
by a shade of criminal that is still sort of hazy
but with clear messages sent to the subliminal
telling US that African't American
when WE know that
southern Jim Crow segregation
and northern migration
led US to an urban ghettoization
and a subsequent racial oppression

all in that succession
with our masses unemployed
and underemployed;
unable for US to avoid,
so, our illegal activities
foster underground economies
and facilitate the American criminal justice system
along with its penal institutions.
Perpetuating our political and civic exclusion
as a nation of African American'ts.
But my people boast
Black nationalists,
revolutionaries,
and social reformists
from Douglass
to DuBois,
and Garvey,
with Mandela,
Malcolm,
and Martin.
Whether considered racists,
supremacists,
or separatists,
they are all considered,
in their own right,
some type of activist.
And in their spirits resurrected,
WE will fight
for Civil Rights
using Black Power
and raised, clenched Black fists
as Pan-African American't nationalists
bringing forth urban disturbance
and inner city insurrections.
Taking US forward in other directions
because wherever American't
African.

With multimillion dollar land deals
being made over land that's adjacent to
hazardous waste dumps and radioactivity
as my people call into AM talk stations
with plenty of radioactivity. Speaking
up and speaking out on underhanded
business agreements made above the board
for US all to plainly see it. As WE call
and WE complain but WE still aint said a
damn thing before the crack moved in,
when US Blacks moved in beyond a 7%
threshold and they labeled it a ghetto
that made our properties worth less
until a point that our property was

RECOGNIZE

Peep Game

...proceed

hate the players

Pathfindin' (4 My 'Hood)

I walk my path
knowing that sometimes I have
the people wondering:
is he *on something,*
on to something,
or *up to something?*
Why is he out in the 'hood?
Is he *up to no good?*
Or is he *up to nothing?*
Why is this so troubling?
Because the same type of 'hood
where I used to live
is where I now choose to live.
And peep this, the evil only exists
where good goes too far off the path.
Although my 'hood may be *a bit too far* off the path,
I wonder, exactly, *how far* is that?
To say, "I know" is understating
because the answer takes some debating.
With multimillion dollar land deals
being made over landfills
adjacent to hazardous waste dumps
and radioactivity
as my people call into AM talk stations
with plenty of radio activity.

Speaking up
and speaking out
on underhanded business agreements
made above the board for US all to plainly see it.
As WE call and WE complain
but WE still ain't said a damn thing
before the crack moved in,
when US Blacks moved in beyond a 7% threshold
and they labeled it a ghetto
to make the property values worth less
until a point that our property was valued as worthless.
So, I ponder as I wander about
wondering about what will become of my 'hood?
What will become of its promise …?
What will become of its people …?
Do urban blight
and suburban flight
provide the sequel
to crack transforming cities into ghost towns
with the remainder either torn up or burned down?
Will abandoned tenements
and failed government housing projects
provide potential prospects for gentrification?
See, my 'hood holds more potential prospects
for more money making
but just not for US
when WE purchase property at market rate
but WE sell as soon as the property values deflate,
allowing the other guy
to come in
and buy low
then sell high.
You see, WE
must embrace and take hold
to stay in control
of the 'hood.

Color My Revolution Black

Power to the People!
Excessively burdened with no equal.
And WE carry our burdens like guns—
Uzis that weigh tons.
Revolution comes as fires carry colors of rage.
With media as the stage—
delayed broadcasts
and now podcast
but originally untelevised.
And if the revolution must have a color,
then I know that
it must be Black.

Final Chapter
(13 of the American
Dream)

America the Beautiful has an ugly ass face.
An ugly ass place.
She fears me.
She hears me and then she says,
"Love it or leave it!"
I wanna love it.
For damn sure ain't gonna be leavin' it.
But for damn sure cain't believe in it.
Hypocrisy …
Democracy …
WE do little with "due diligence"
then claim ignorance.
Politicians step out into the foreground taking …
constituents' in the background sounds making …
Ground breaking?
Or just background noise
accompanying plenty of games
played like political toys.
Saw those same old faces
but seen them for the first time
locked away in strange places.
The same as mine.
Until I took control of my life.

Put the soul on ice.
Stepped out onto the front lines
to reclaim what was once mine.
Got down with the home team.
RED, BLACK, and GREEN!
Raised the flag
as I raised my fist
and raised my socio-political consciousness
from that of a mis-educated Negro.
Vaingloriously; in honor of our fallen heroes
like Black Americans making a covenant
for the brothers and sisters struggling
but barely making it.
So unbearable at times WE barely are taking it.
Disenfranchised from the American dream
as a nightmarish reality
birthed for US a militant mentality.
And as WE newfound mental militants
hear the voices of resistance,
WE make life long decisions in an instant.
From a doctrine of separate but equal
to proclaiming "Power to the People!"
And ain't no small wonder
how cold winters in America
become long, hot summers.

Almighty ME

I and I.

Just Me,
Myself,
and I.

My 3rd eye shines visionary
as pilgrimages return US back to Mecca;
back to a life viewed in its proper perspective.
Not eyewitness news accounts on CBS with no say so
but with the all seeing eye of Ra that guided the pharaohs.

All mighty because I am faithful.

No need to discuss, debate, or
argue being one with the creator
because I am all mighty
and I am blessed with
a suggested
oneness.

All mighty.

Me.

Revolution: does it always mean revolting, or does it sometimes mean revolving? Involving WE who have the least to lose but the most to prove. Global warfare and conflict fought by young and poor men although is old, rich men who started it. Those in control and planning, in the background standing by. Pushing buttons. Talking loud but saying nothing. The story a catastrophe. But is

(2 Much of the Same)
A Game Theory

A humble servant's choice to preach
but through ghetto tones
urban voices speak.
Because once I publish it
becomes anonymous.
So, my poetic verses performed become spoken word
or slam artistry when interjected with that verb.
The interjection of some local color
into this introspection from a vocal brother,
and you may hear me say "ain't",
or you might hear me say "cain't",
"I be" or "we gon'"
'cause after all we's Black folks ... so its on.
Now, The Almighty blessed US with one mouth
and two ears to share our concerns.
Our ears with which WE listen and WE learn.
The mouth by which WE speak and WE teach.
As WE preach,
WE should listen twice as much as WE speak
but instead WE hear only half of what WE say.
WE pray
and WE imposition
our thoughts, our beliefs, as well as our positions
on what is considered as a respectable behavior
to be acceptable to our Savior.

But WE won't do it ourselves.
Holier than thou but on our way straight towards Hell.
Like the Grim Reaper,
our brother's keeper steals food from his table.
Crime—
Black on Black
can be traced back to Cain and Abel.
But as WE opened our eyes, our echoed cries
got heard in every ghetto zone
and every urbanized area reached.
Like I said before, through ghetto tones
the urban voices speak.
Y'all know what I mean!
WE threw a monkey wrench in the machine
and WE put things to the test
through civil unrest
because breaking the silence of the ghetto
awakens the violence of the ghetto.
Internalized and displaced in the aftermath of questionable police beatings.
Following orders from the old heads also known as the street kings.
"To arms!" goes out the call to all of the young urban warriors
while "stand at the ready" is told to all of our jailhouse lawyers.
Now they cain't figure out how it got this way
as some folks note, "Yo! Dat nigga got a lot to say!"
or "Peep out how m'man gets ..."
Just check on my transcript:
Idolized
through some eyes.
Broken down and ionized to
I and I
as a Conquering Lion of Judah,
a son of Islam,
a child of Israel,
or a soldier for Christ.
No matter—traveling the enlightened path.
Seeking The Light.
Battled alcoholism
along with racism.

As I educated my community,
I was soon to see the face of classism.
Called "unprofessional"
or "just plain ghetto"
by some who never knew me.
By others, I got called "borghese".
An "ordinary nigga"
put up on a pedestal
then held up to a higher level.
But what is it?
I really am no different.
Saying the same thing
while playing the same game.
Sometimes talking loud but saying nothing.
Sometimes saying something.
Or having something to say
while they're running away from me
and my spoken word artistry …
my ghetto tone …
my urban voice.
It may be their choice to not accept it as a part of me.
But they can't except it as a part from me
and they can't expect it to depart from me.

978-0-595-46056-4
0-595-46056-9